MAKING
JOURNALS
BY HAND

26 creative projects for keeping your thoughts

BY JASON THOMPSON

ROCKPORT

Thank you to **the artists** who were kind enough to let us take peek into their private journals. To Lori Kay who was supportive from the start. Roz and Bruce whose quick and encouraging replies to eMail were pleasantly received.

Thanks to the talented and creative **Rockport staff:** Martha for the opportunity, Cathy for the art direction and Jay for the inspiration.

Thanks to the **Rag & Bone Bindery** crew: Rae, Jes, Val, Kim, Sandy, Robert, Joe, Anne & Bob and the rest for the flexibility to spend four pre-occupied months on this project.

To my **family:** Janet, John, Doris and Marty for your support.

To my good **friends:** Amy and Cassandra from Rugg Road Paper Company for the reference and creative influences, to Fredrik and Joe for being positive and creative friendship. And especially to my wonderful wife Ilira for your continuing support and respect.

Jason Thompson
Winter, 2000

Copyright © 2000 by Rockport Publishers, Inc.

First published in the United States of America by
Rockport Publishers, Inc.
33 Commercial Street
Gloucester, Massachusetts   01930-5089
Telephone: (978) 282-9590
Facsimile: (978) 283-2742
www.rockpub.com

ISBN 1-56496-676-3
10 9 8 7 6 5 4

Art Direction and Photo Styling: Cathy Kelley
Design: Lynn Faitelson
Cover Image and Interior Photography: Kevin Thomas

"Choosing Your Paper," (see pages 10–11), by Megan Fitzpatrick, originally appeared in the magazine *Personal Journaling*, from F&W Publications. For more information on this magazine, call 1-800-289-0963 or visit www.journalingmagazine.com.

Printed in China.

Contents

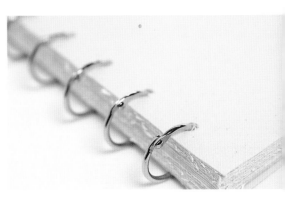

Introduction

Welcome to *Making Journals by Hand.* You are holding one of the first books of its kind to peek inside the personal journals of writers, artists, and creative types. Among these pages you will find examples of daily journals, artists' sketchbooks, travel journals, historical journals, and more, dating from the middle eighteenth century to the present day. You will also find journal-keeping lessons and projects to follow along with.

Faithfully keeping a journal is an art, a craft, a discipline, a ritual, and, for many journal keepers, a release—a conduit for the ideas, inspiration, experiences, and dreams that flow in and out of our daily lives. The techniques vary, but the inspiration is universal. The process of creating and keeping visual journals is a way to say those things that don't get said in every day life. The insight we experience in quiet moments can gain strength and permanence when put to page. Our personal communication can lead to growth, change, and self-awareness, or just as importantly, simply serve as a memory of a time and place to look back to later on in life. While some journalers find it difficult to start a new book, others are sure to keep at least one fresh, blank journal handy at all times. Many journal keepers create their own hand-bound books, and this book will teach and describe several book-making techniques.

Visual journals are more than diaries. At their most extravagant, visual journals are filled with words, photographs, found objects, collages, newspaper clippings, rubber stamps, postage stamps—you name it. A journal may also be dedicated to a specific theme or event in one's life, such as travel or gardening. A journal doesn't necessarily have to even be a book with pages, as seen in some of the examples in this book.

This is not to say that journals can't contain the mundane or that they have to be pretty or confessional. Garden journals, travel journals, and wedding journals are a few of the themed books that allow writers, gardeners, and travelers to open up and record their specific thoughts and memories. Where did I plant the parsley last year? Who did we visit on our trip to New Mexico? Or better yet, why did I plant parsley and not basil? Or, what was I thinking, visiting New Mexico in July?

When I look back at the daily minutia and wisdom I have documented in my own journals, I feel lucky to have preserved the memories of those thoughts, places, and people. I'm able to look back and read about the ideas I had five and ten years ago. I can relive those same emotions,

recall the faces of the people I have lost touch with, remember the dreams I had, and reflect on the development of my own skills of writing, drawing, and collage, which I still practice today.

This book will describe several visual journal-keeping techniques, such as creating image transfers from photo-graphs and hand-carving individual rubber stamps. It will also explore other artistic themes that complement the written word, such as techniques for keeping a memorable travel journal. Finally, you will find a gallery of journals that are confessional, inspired, and beautiful.

As the contents of journals are as individual as their creators, we'll leave the writing to you. If you need motivation, many books contain exercises and examples for you to follow along with to assist with creative writing techniques. See the bibliography for more information.

I hope you can find inspiration within these pages to start or continue your own personal history. It may sound clichéd, but there's no better time to begin creating your journal than the present.

Jason Thompson
Rag & Bone Bindery
Winter 2000

The author's journal making box contains an assortment of tools. You can create your own custom decorated box to store all of your findings and materials.

Materials List

JOURNALING SUPPLIES Every journaler uses, at minimum, a blank book and a pen or pencil. Some journalers have favorite fountain pens or particular styles of books they like to use. Or they make their own one-of–a-kind books, such as those described and show-cased in later chapters. Many other supplies are useful for creating and designing journals. Keeping a journal box (as seen on the introduction page) is a creative way to store and personalize your own journal-keeping materials.

BOOKBINDING SUPPLIES Certain tools and materials are required to hand-bind books. Some of the materials listed here can be replaced by others—you can, for example, make your own book cloth— but it's a good idea to have a sturdy glue brush, a bone folder, and appropriate adhesives on hand (especially PVA glue, a bookbinding glue) when making books.

ART MATERIALS AND SUPPLIES Now-adays you can purchase many different craft materials and art supplies at nation-ally franchised art and craft superstores. The resources section in the back of the book also lists Internet and mail-order

1. blank book ballpoint, fountain, or dip pens
2. inks pencils, erasers, markers, crayons
3. spray adhesive, glue stick, or PVA glue
4. tape 5. scissors 6. binder's tape 7. bone folder 8. matte knife 9. ruler 10. glue brush
11. needle and thread 12. awl 13. screw posts
14. clasps 15. beads 16. leather lacing 17. gesso
18. paint brush 19. xylene and other solvents
20. respirator or dust mask 21. spackle and knife 22. hole punch or drill 23. candy thermometer 24. spray enamel 25. brayer
26. carving tools 27. sand paper or sanding block

supply companies, from which you can buy artists' materials such as those listed here and throughout the book.

OTHER TOOLS, SUPPLIES, AND MATERIALS The tools and materials listed here, some of which you may already have in your home or studio, are used in many of the projects in the book. Be sure to read and follow any manufacturer's warnings before using chemicals such as solvents and adhesives.

Choosing Your Paper

All paper is not created equal. Yes, you could write in 39¢ school notebooks, but your journal should be recorded on a medium that will endure. Before you go out and buy reams of paper or a bound book of blank pages for your journal, try this inexpensive and relatively quick experiment to evaluate paper quality: Collect the morning paper from your front step (or neighbor's bushes, as the case may be), and after you've read it, leave a page sitting in direct sunlight. By dinner time, that page will already be yellowing, and you will have found that not all paper is meant to last. Up until the mid 1800s, paper was composed of cellulose fiber derived from old rags and linen, and bleached with lime, which is highly alkaline. The lime also served as a buffering agent, protecting the paper from external acid introduction, such as handling by human hands. But by the Civil War, the demand for paper out-

stripped the supply of linen and rags, and new ingredients for paper-making had to be found.

The main ingredient in most modern paper is wood pulp, and the processes developed for bleaching, sizing (which waterproofs the paper to some extent to keep ink from bleeding) and finishing this paper involves a lot of highly acidic chemicals, which cause the paper to break down over time. This is why all those paperback books from your childhood are now falling apart. And the more you handled them; the more acid you introduced through the oils in your skin, further causing deterioration.

THE RIGHT STUFF

The main thing to look for when selecting paper for your journal is acid-free paper. Fifteen years ago, it was hard to find high-quality acid-free writing paper, but now almost every decent bookstore carries at least a few bound blank books of acid-free pages. These may cost a few dollars more than the acidic variety, but if you want people to be able to read your words in the future, it's worth the investment. Plus, to further assuage your guilt over spending the extra money, the processes used in producing acid-free paper are more environmentally friendly. Manufacturing acid-free paper produces fewer run-off contaminants, and the product usually includes some recycled content. If you prefer to

write at your computer, acid-free printer paper is also available. But remember to print your pages from time to time. After all, in a few more years, floppy disks may be museum pieces! For more information and sources on where to find archival products such as acid-free paper and journals, see the Resources section at the end of this book.

PRESERVATION NO-NO'S

Even if the paper you're using is of the best quality, acid and other destructive factors can be introduced inadvertently. Glue, binding cloth, staples and threads commonly used to hold books together can have disastrous effects on the longevity of your work. While there may not be too much you can do about these bad influences, here are some things you can easily avoid.

CLIPPINGS: Try to avoid introducing newspaper clippings into your journal pages, as the acid will migrate from the low-quality newsprint to your relatively expensive, high-quality pages, making it money ill-spent. Instead, copy clippings onto acid-free paper.

ACCESSORIES: Avoid using paper clips, rubber bands and self-adhesive notes as they can cause permanent damage to your pages. Even most inks can introduce harmful acid onto your paper, although for a small investment, you can buy ballpoint pens with acid-free inks.

OTHER DETRIMENTS: Light (especially UV), animals (including mice, cockroaches, silverfish, bookworms and your dog), food and drink, heat above 70 degrees (60 is safer, but rather limiting), and humidity are all environmental factors destructive to paper.

AVOIDING DAMAGE

If your goal is to make your writing last, even the right combination of paper, binding materials and ink alone won't preserve your journal for future generations. The manner in which you treat your journal also contributes to its longevity. Don't fold the page corners over to mark your place and don't use the book as a coaster for your morning coffee. Don't write in the bathtub (at least, don't write in the journal you want to save in the bathtub). Finally, once you've completed a volume, store it in a cool, dark dry place that is easy to clean... and (we hate to say it) clean there once in awhile. The best way to store your completed volumes is to keep them in archival quality (acid-free) boxes. Don't keep them in wooden chests as the chests can become infested, or in metal boxes, unless they're specially made for archival storage, as the boxes may corrode.

Blank Books

A blank book is the starting point for just about every journal showcased in this book. On the right are unused blank books, ranging from one-of-a-kind, leather-covered, hand-bound journals, to store-bought, spiral-bound notebooks and just about every variation in between. The recent revival of diary-writing and journal-keeping has created a market for journals, which are now available just about everywhere, from your local arts supply store to stationery boutiques, craft fairs, and even your corner drugstore. Many of the blank books shown here are created by the same artists whose work is featured throughout the rest of this book.

Historical Journals

A rich history of personal, hand-written diaries begins with the earliest known manuscript dairy, the *Kagero Diary*, written by a Japanese woman in the tenth century, to well-known published diaries such as *The Diary of Anne Frank* and the diaries of Anaïs Nin. Visual journals are similar to diaries in that they're confessional and personal, but they also contain more than daily written entries. Your local bookstore sells fully reprinted visual journals, such as *Spilling Open: The Art of Becoming Yourself* by Sabrina Ward Harrison and *The Journey Is the Destination: The Journals of Dan Eldon*. These are facsimile journals—actual reprints—containing exquisitely embellished journal pages similar to the journals featured in this book.

The history of visual journals is not well documented, but collectors of diaries and historical journals are aware of books with unusual contents that date to the mid-1800s, when the first diaries filled with more than written entries began to appear. Here is a small gallery containing examples of these visual diaries of historical note that are the pre-decessors to current journal keepers' books.

ABOVE, AND FACING PAGE, TOP: From the collection of Sally Mac Namara-Ivey & Kevin Ivey. FACING PAGE, BOTTOM: Handwritten account of a woman's trip to Europe in the summer of 1897, which discusses life aboard the Ocean Liners "La Champagne" and the "Kaiser Wilhelm" as well as travels in Europe. From the collection of Sally Mac Namara-Ivey & Kevin Ivey.

BELOW: One of "Self-Taught" artist James Castle's journals circa 1930's, "BLAW Book" challenges the concept of the codex format and contains stylized rendered scenes and illustrations. Courtesy of a private collector. RIGHT: A young woman's hand-written diary and scrapbook of her trip from Longport to Chicago's Worlds Fair including a visit to Niagara Falls and the city of Chicago. From the collection of Sally Mac Namara-Ivey & Kevin Ivey. BOTTOM: A diary kept by Alice Bentley onboard the ship "Normandie" which begins in New York City and ends in LeHavre with photos and mementos. From the collection of Sally Mac Namara-Ivey & Kevin Ivey

LEFT: 200 handwritten pages from a record book with partial diary entries dating from the 1790's. Includes an interesting entry about General George Washington's death. From the collection of Sally Mac Namara-Ivey & Kevin Ivey. BELOW: This book contains over 100 personal and business letters received by a young man just graduated from Yale University who spends his summer sketching and trying to sell his sketches. From the collection of Sally Mac Namara-Ivey & Kevin Ivey.

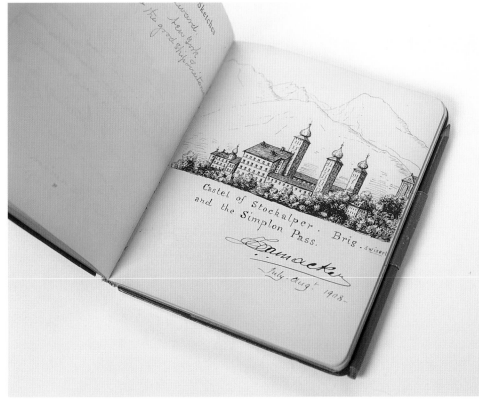

ABOVE: Contains an account of a trip to England and other parts of Europe on board the ship "Lusitania" with records of places visited including lunch with Lord and Lady Furness. From the collection of Sally Mac Namara-Ivey & Kevin Ivey. MIDDLE RIGHT: This book contains ten handwritten autographed poetry pieces dating from 1845–1848, each with braided hair pieces of each author. From the collection of Sally Mac Namara-Ivey & Kevin Ivey. BOTTOM RIGHT: "Nellies Ledger" Created from a ledger belonging to the sister of Self-Taught artist James Castle. Narratives and patterns are created by collages of found illustrations pasted on pages covered with a wash of soot and saliva ink. Courtesy Private Collector.

Journal Projects

Some visual journals are created spontaneously, while others are crafted with purpose. Whether you have predetermined creative ideas or not, your journals will probably contain quite a bit of flotsam and jetsam, including stickers, stamps, postcards, pictures, ticket stubs, newspaper clippings—you name it. Creating order from a chaotic wellspring of ideas and inspiration requires some planning—and, most of all, some inspiration.

With specific themes, your journals can focus your artistic ideas. Whether you create a garden, recipe, or travel journal, use your one-of-a kind journals as containers for your own personal spirit and individual vision.

Following are several journal projects for you to work along with. Use these projects to create your own themed journals or simply as motivation and creative inspiration.

Making Your Own Journals

So you want to keep a journal. Many wonderful blank journals are available from your local stationery, gift, and arts and crafts stores. Bookbinders also sometimes sell blank books to small local shops in the communities where they live and work. Visit a university bookstore or independent bookseller near you to find small-run, individually created blank books. You may also look at arts and crafts shows—anywhere bookbinders might sell their work.

But if you're ready to make your own journal, here are three examples of simple books you can create without much experience or bookbinding skills. In addition, an extensive bibliography at the end of this book offers recommendations for detailed bookbinding tutorial publications.

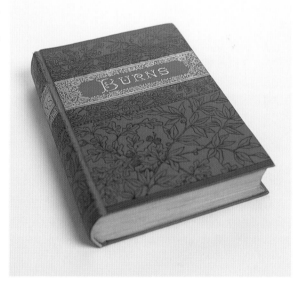

Creating a Spiral-Bound Book

MATERIALS

writing paper

decorative paper

other ephemera
such as envelopes,
handmade paper,
printed pages,
mailing and label
tags, photographs,
post cards, etc.

To create your own personal journal, let's
start with a very simple technique that
requires no bookbinding experience or
special knowledge. Many journalers write
and create in spiral-bound journals, as
seen throughout this book, instead of
case-bound journals for two reasons:
They can lay the journal flat without
stressing its spine, and the spiral binding
allows items to be added within their
pages without the book "yawning" open
when it is closed. Creating your own spiral-bound book can actually be less expensive than buying one in the store. But
most importantly, creating your own
allows you the freedom to add unique elements such as printed pages, envelopes,
decorative papers, and different colored
sheets into the binding.

ONE

**STEP ONE GATHER AND COLLATE YOUR
PAGES** Gather the pages and other items
you plan to have bound into your new book
and collate them into the correct order. You can
use a binder clip to hold the pages together
until just prior to binding. Most service
bureaus can fit up to an inch of material in
their spiral-binding machines and can even
accept heavy card stock or bookbinding
board for the front and back covers.

TWO

STEP TWO SPIRAL-BIND YOUR BOOK
You will need to locate a service bureau that
has the equipment necessary to spiral-bind
books and booklets. Most local copy centers have this equipment, and many service
bureaus will create your book while you
wait. From start to finish, your book can
be created in an afternoon!

Rebinding a Store-Bought Journal

MATERIALS

drawing paper

needle

thread

Maybe you've already found a style of journal that you like, but it isn't exactly what you need for every occasion. Maybe you like to use watercolors on some pages, and pens and pencils on others. Wouldn't it be great to have a book that had water-color paper on some pages, and lined or unlined writing paper on others? With this simple re-binding technique, you can deconstruct a single-signature binding to create a book for all occasions. In order to rebind a store-bought book as described in these steps, you'll need a one-signature book, also known as a pamphlet. A signature is a group of pages that are folded in half and sewn along the fold to hold the pages together. One-signature journals contain only one group of pages sewn together in the middle. You can sometimes find these types of books stapled instead of sewn. Either type of book will work for this project.

STEP ONE **DISASSEMBLE THE PAGES**
Remove the thread or staples that hold the book together. The holes in the fold of the pages will be used when re-sewing the pages back together. Add new pages, such as colored sheets, printed pages from a computer, or thicker paper for drawing, to the signature of old pages.

STEP TWO **REBIND THE PAGES**   When the new pages have been added into the signature, use a needle to punch holes through these new sheets to correspond to the rest of the holes in the original signature. Sew your reconstructed signature and the original cover, if there was one, together with a needle and thread. Tightly tie the ends of the thread together inside the signature in the middle of the book, and you're ready to write!

Rebinding a Vintage Book

MATERIALS

writing paper

decorative paper

razor

PVA glue

glue brush

damp rag

sandpaper

This is the most difficult of the three projects, but it's also the most fun! With this simple technique, you can bind your own individual blank book with any vintage book cover of your choice.

ONE

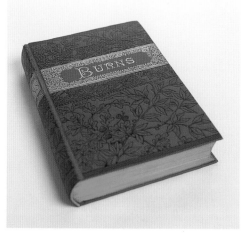

STEP ONE GATHER THE MATERIALS
Begin by locating a hardcover book with an interesting cover. Try used book stores, library book sales, and flea markets. Next, gather your new pages. Experiment with different writing papers, as some types of papers are opaque, while others are transparent; some papers are durable enough to take artists' materials, some are best used for writing only. It may be a good idea to attempt this project with a book that is smaller than 8.5" x 11" (22cm x 28cm), a standard-size sheet of writing paper, so you will be able to find paper readily from retail paper vendors and copy centers.

TWO

STEP TWO DISASSEMBLE THE BOOK
Carefully remove the book block—all the pages inside the book—from the cover by slicing along the folds between the book block and the cover, being careful not to cut the cover. You should have two items when you're finished, the book block and the cover, which consists of the front cover, the spine, and the back cover. Here's a tip: Some books have spines that are glued to the book block and thus are not appropriate for this project. If you can look down through the spine from the top of the book when it's held open, you've got the right kind of binding. Professional bookbinders will completely remove the endsheets (the heavy paper glued to the inside of the covers) before rebinding a book. If you're not comfortable disassembling the covers entirely, simply use sandpaper to smooth any frayed ends or loose glue along the cover's inside edges.

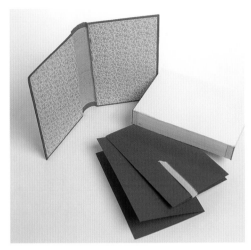
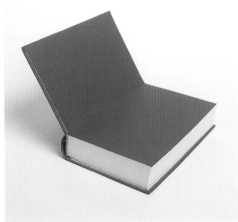

STEP THREE **CREATE A NEW BOOK BLOCK** Carefully measure the removed book block and write down its thickness, length, and width. Once you have decided on a type of paper for the pages of your book, assemble as many sheets as it takes to create a stack that is as thick as your original vintage book. Take this stack and the book's measurements to your service bureau and ask them to perfect-bind your sheets—glue the sheets together along one edge to create a new spine—and cut them down to the exact size as the old book block. When it is done, you will have a new book block the same size as the one you removed but containing blank pages.

STEP FOUR **REBIND THE BOOK** Here's the fun part! Gather two thick sheets of paper to be used as your endsheets. Your new endsheets should be the same length as your new book block but twice as wide. When these sheets are folded in half, they should be the same width and length as your book block. Place a strip of a PVA-type glue approximately one inch wide along the folded edges of the new end-sheets, and glue them to the book block so that the folds of the endsheets are adjacent to the spine. Next, carefully cover the entire outer side of the endsheet with glue and press the new book block into the old cov-ers. Remove any stray glue with a damp rag. As most of us don't have a book press handy, you can stack a pile of books or something heavy such as bricks on top of your newly glued book. Allow it to dry overnight.

Daily Journals

MATERIALS

writing pages

decorative paper

awl

needle

thread

beads (optional)

Daily journals are the most common and flexible journals. Daily journals contain diary entries, wisdom, everyday minutia, and ephemera collected from daily life such as ticket stubs, labels, stickers, business cards, and photographs. There are as many formats of daily journals as there are journalers, but there are a few common elements, such as pictures of pets and the ubiquitous coffee-cup ring. Artist Wendy Hale Davis keeps beautiful daily journals, and, being a professional book-binder, she even binds her own exquisite, leather-bound books. They contain daily entries, Wendy's beautiful handwritten calligraphic headings, and items and objects glued onto the pages.

I STARTED KEEPING JOURNALS IN 1970 BECAUSE MY BOYFRIEND AT THE TIME DID. OVER TIME MY BOOKS HAVE BECOME MORE INTENTIONAL AND ARTISTIC.

Artist: Wendy Hale Davis

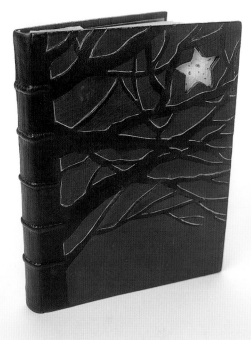

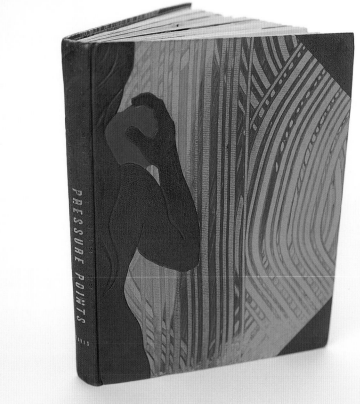

Step by Step:

ONE

TWO

THREE

STEP ONE **FOLD THE SIGNATURE AND COVER MATERIAL**   A one-signature book is a very easy way to begin making your own books. Begin by folding four or five writing pages in half to form a single signature. Then fold decorative paper in half to make the cover.

STEP TWO **SEW THE SINGLE SIGNATURE**   Use an awl to pre-punch holes into the crease or spine of your book. We have pre-punched five holes in our example and used embroidery floss that we have coated with beeswax to prevent knotting. Begin sewing through the spine from the top and outside of the book down through to the bottom hole, then sew back up again to the top hole. Tie the two loose ends together tightly.

STEP THREE **EMBELLISH WITH BEADS** Tie beads onto the loose ends of the thread for a decorative element.

notes:

Make your daily journal out of sturdy material. It will be used quite a bit.

To prompt yourself to create and write something in your journal on a regular basis, date the pages.

Use your daily journal as a place to work out ideas for themed books, such as garden or recipe journals.

After many, many years have passed, long after you're gone, your journals will be read by friends or family members. Think about writing down the personal stories from your life that only you will remember. Think of all the times you say to someone, "I remember back when ... " and transcribe these stories into your journal. They will be priceless to the people who come after you.

TOP LEFT AND BOTTOM RIGHT: This journal was collaged by Dorothy Krause with materials collected on a two week trip to Vietnam. BOTTOM LEFT: Judy Serebrin kept this journal in Cambridge, England, to earn credits for a master of fine arts degree.
TOP RIGHT: Dorothy Krause remembers a year she taught at the Massachusetts College of Art in Boston with this book.

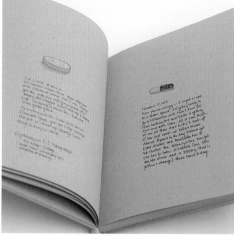

TOP LEFT: Kez van Oudheusden's visual journal of an academic semester. LEFT AND TOP RIGHT: Two books by Marilyn Reaves. ABOVE: Roz Stendahl's "Things to Do Until I See You Again."

ABOVE: A daily journal by Judy Serebrin. ABOVE
RIGHT: Narratives and drawings from a time when
Jeffree Stewart worked as a river guide in Northern
New Mexico. RIGHT: Judy Serebrin's "Israel Journal I."

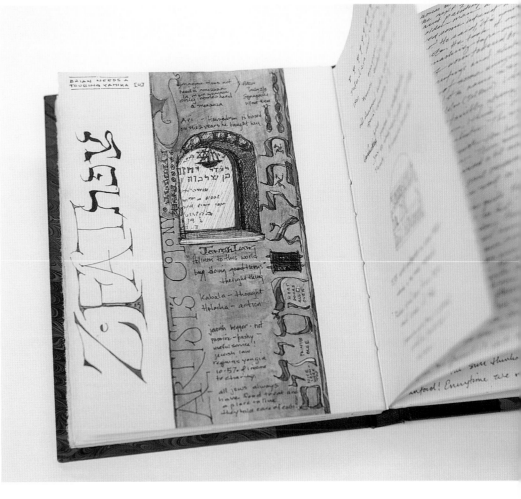

Travel Journals

MATERIALS

pen

pencil

watercolors

paint brush

glue stick

tape

kneaded eraser

razor

**a Swiss army knife
and a flashlight may
also come in handy**

Travel journals are probably the most inspirational way to keep a visual journal. We all want to remember our memories of visiting new places and meeting new people. Keeping a journal while you are travelling and while your experiences are still fresh in your mind seems to be a natural thing to do. Bruce Kremer has been keeping travel journals for twenty years, filling over a dozen of them in that time. Travel journals often contain common elements, and we will discuss three of them in detail.

MY TRAVEL JOURNAL CONTAINS WRITTEN ENTRIES,

COLLAGES, AND DAILY OCCURRENCES.

Artist: Bruce Kremer

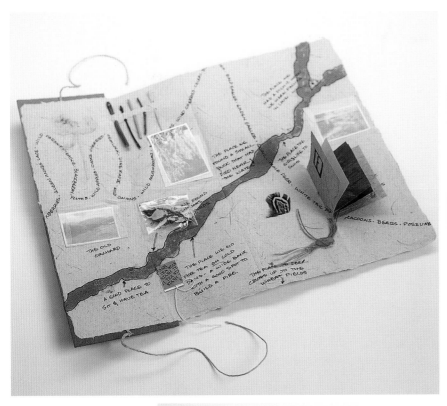

TOP LEFT: Elizabeth Clark deconstructed a childhood geography book and reassembled it, including etchings, photocopied images and handmade paper. TOP RIGHT, BOTTOM LEFT AND RIGHT: Artist: Bruce Kremer

Step by Step:

ONE

TWO

THREE

ABOVE LEFT: This book is filled with ephemera and scraps recording events which Bruce Kremer has incorporated with written entries to remember his journey. ABOVE RIGHT: The pages of Bruce Kremer's travel journals embody places visited and people met through collected and layered mementos and the written word. LEFT: This book records Bruce Kremer's around-the-world trip taken in 1991 and features written entries and found ephemera and mementos attached to the page. FACING PAGE, TOP: While traveling in Morocco, Evelyn Eller remembered buying an old Koran in Istanbul and thought that the pages from that book would make an ideal background for this travel journal. FACING PAGE, MIDDLE: Cheryl Slyter created this journal after a trip to Spain and France in April, 1999. She bound photos printed on Arches Test Wove paper as the, "…tactile quality of the paper is delightful." FACING PAGE, BOTTOM LEFT AND RIGHT: This book was created to be both a reference and notebook/sketchbook for Laura Blacklow's visit to Dallas. Each board is covered with half of the inner city map.

STEP ONE **COLLECT PAPER ITEMS AND OTHER EPHEMERA** Be sure to collect paper ephemera that can be added to your journal, such as postage stamps, local wine and beer labels, ticket stubs, currency, cigarette packs, candy wrappers, receipts, and especially handwritten notes, directions, or letters in local script. Keep your glue stick, knife, or tape handy.

STEP TWO **PLOT AND RECORD YOUR PROGRESS** Look for local maps, which can make great backgrounds for journal pages. You can also plot your progress with comments and memories of your own experiences right on the maps.

STEP THREE **NO CAMERA? DRAW IT!** Probably the most common element found in travel journals is photographs. But if you didn't bring a camera with you, a drawing is the next best thing. Use colored pencils, crayons, and even ballpoint pens to sketch what's around you.

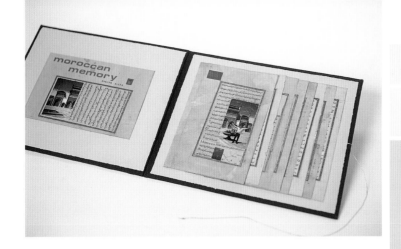

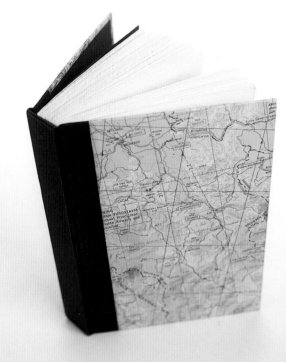

A journal is a blank book just waiting for your creative input. It can be kept as memento of a place, time, or event. Here are examples of journals with different themes that can be used to facilitate writing:

GARDEN JOURNAL Document daily memories from tending or creating gardens

DREAM JOURNAL Record nightly dreams

TRAVEL JOURNAL Chronicle your travels

BABY JOURNAL Start during pregnancy, and continue after the birth of a new baby

WEDDING JOURNAL Document the time from an engagement to a wedding

ANNIVERSARY JOURNAL Record special recurring events

FAMILY JOURNAL Remember your family for the next generation with pictures and anecdotes

WINE JOURNAL Keep track of the wine you drink, and include the labels

READING JOURNAL Write about the books you've read

QUILTING JOURNAL Catalog family quilts, and include fabric swatches and pictures

ACTIVITY JOURNAL Describe a favorite hobby or sport

DAILY JOURNAL Document your daily life with words and pictures

RECIPE JOURNAL Keep a list of personal recipes, and include pictures of food, meals, and friends

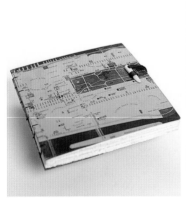

notes:

Ask customs officials or local postal employees to stamp your journal.

If something you want to include is too heavy or too thick, use a blender pen to transfer a photocopy of it.

Save leaves and flowers to press into your journal. Make leaf impressions or use clear tape to completely tape in a flower.

Recipe Journals

MATERIALS

**card stock or
watercolor paper**

decorative paper

ribbon

needle

hole punch or drill

glue

scissors

photocorners

Simply put, a recipe journal is a book that contains recipes. But along with simple cooking instructions, a recipe journal may also document the cooking process, contain pictures of meals with friends, and include food labels and comments about favorite recipes. By personalizing a journal with handwritten notes, instructions, and comments, a recipe journal can become a family heirloom. Artist Anne Woods created a recipe journal to remember meals shared with good neighbors before moving across country. She shares not only her recipes but her thoughts, impressions, photographs, and drawings of her neighbors in this one-of-a-kind book.

I CREATED THIS JOURNAL FOR MY NEIGHBOURS AND GOOD FRIENDS, TO COMMEMORATE RECIPES AND MEALS WE HAVE SHARED TOGETHER.

Artist: Anne Woods

Artist: Anne Woods

Step by Step:

RECIPE JOURNALS

STEP ONE   **GATHER THE MATERIALS**   Pre-cut the card stock or watercolor paper to a uniform size. Gather your pictures, recipes, decorative papers, and other elements to include in your recipe journal.

STEP TWO   **CREATE THE PAGES**   Create your pages as individual pieces. Glue recipes to the pre-cut cardstock or watercolor paper, attach pictures of meals or wine labels, record your thoughts about meals with good friends, and even jot personal notes and hints about certain recipes. Each piece of cardstock should be a two-sided page, with elements on both the front and back. As each page is a single piece, experiment with laying them out in different orders before you bind them in. And remember to leave room at the edges of your pages for the holes and ribbon!

STEP THREE   **BIND THE PAGES TOGETHER** Create a front and back cover with card-stock or watercolor paper. At the same spot on each of the cards, punch or drill two large holes. Slip a ribbon-threaded needle through each hole and tie with a decorative bow.

When writing in your journal, don't forget to write about the people around you, your family and friends. You may think now that a short visit by a distant relative isn't something to write about, but a hundred years from now, your future relatives may think differently. Think about what you would find interesting if you could read your great-grandmother or grandfathers journals. What was a typical day like? It may seem trite, but what does a loaf of bread cost? A first-class stamp? Why not place a first-class stamp into your journal? Take a picture of your home or your family, date your entries, and be sure to write somewhere in the front of your journal, "This book belongs to ..." with a date and, if possible, a picture of yourself.

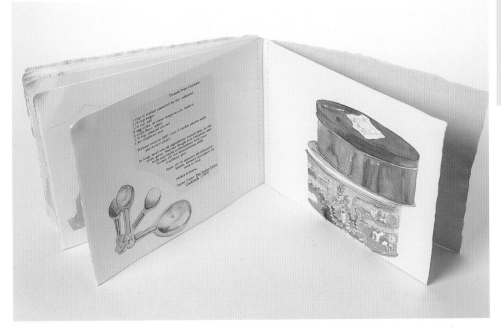

Katy Gilmore created this book to honor the everyday. It contains embellished, meaningful quotes; journal writing; and everyday observations.

notes:

Transcribe recipes from older family members. You may be surprised to know what goes into Grandma's meatloaf!

Take pictures of meals to remember good food and good friends.

Save interesting wine and food labels.

Garden Journals

MATERIALS

writing pages

decorative paper cover

hole punch or drill

screw posts

ribbon

leaves

inks

rubber stamps

decorative paper card
(optional)

A garden journal is a book kept to record the daily memories of tending or creating a garden. It contains entries such as a layout of your garden; actual plant material such as leaves, petals, or seeds; daily or weekly entries as to the progress of your garden; and tips, ideas, or wisdom gained from tending gardens. Artist Sherri Keisel created her journal, "A Gardner Reflects," after she had collected items from her gardening experience, but it's just as easy to create the book beforehand and add entries as you're inspired. The type of journal Sherri uses is perfect for a garden journal, which can become soiled from the wear and tear of working and writing in a garden. It is also expandable, which is a great feature for adding gardening mementos to the pages without making the book "yawn" when it is filled.

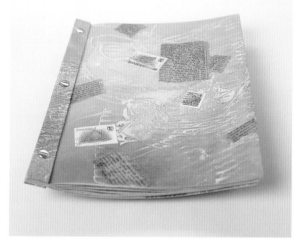

I WANTED TO CAPTURE THE CYCLE OF SEASONS AND THE DEPTH OF TEXTURES OF NATURE ENCOUNTERED IN A GARDENER'S LIFE THROUGH COLOR, TEXT AND ILLUSTRATION.

Artist: Sherri Keisel

THIS PAGE: Sherri Keisel wanted to capture, with color, text and illustration, the cycle of seasons and the depth of textures in the surrounding nature encountered in a gardener's life.

Step by Step:

CREATING A DURABLE, SCREW-POST GARDEN JOURNAL

ONE

TWO

THREE

STEP ONE **ASSEMBLE YOUR MATERIALS**
Collect your pages, cover material, and
any other items you wish to bind into
your book. In this example, we're using a
hand-made, decorative heavyweight writing
paper for the cover.

STEP TWO **CREATE THE COVER** In
our example, we've attached a decorative
card with a leaf impression onto the cover
and used a rubber-stamp alphabet set to
write "Garden Journal."

STEP THREE **BIND THE BOOK!** When
the covers are designed, use either a hole
punch or a drill to create holes in the
binding for the screw posts. To finish the
book off, weave ribbon through the spine
so the book can be hung from a peg or
nail in a garden shed or greenhouse.

notes:

Bind envelopes into the book to
hold seeds of favorite plants.

Create a very personalized decorative
cover for your garden journal by
making your own paper, adding leaves
and petals you have saved from your
garden to the pulp.

Screw posts come in different colors
and patinas, so investigate the possi-
bilities and choose one that's best for
you. For a more industrial look, you
can also use a machine bolt and nut.

The inspiration for Janis Cheek's "Gail's Garden" journal was her best friend's beautiful flower garden and how it changed throughout the summer and fall.

You may find keeping a journal to be a singular experience. Some people find that the most inspiring reason to keep a journal is to share them with others. You might enjoy hearing what friends think about the pages you've created, and you might be surprised by what they like or don't comment about. To gather inspiration from fellow journalers, find out where they get together, or form your own group. The Internet is a wonderful resource for bringing like-minded people together. When you discover communities of other journalers who share the same passions as you do, you might find yourself creating more often. The next time you write or create in your journal, remember that at any given time there are thousands of people all over the world also sitting down to their own personal journals.

Artists' Sketchbooks

MATERIALS

heavyweight pages

hole punch or drill

metal ring clasps

leather laces

beads

needle

thread (optional)

Artists' sketchbooks have existed for a long time. It may be fair to say that they are the true precursor to both diaries and journals. Early examples are Leonardo Da Vinci's "Codex Leicester" notebooks, dating from the early sixteenth century. His sketchbooks document the artist's process of creation in a way his finished works never could. Similarly, twentieth-century artists such as Tracy Moore use sketchbooks as a venue to create their own ideas in an intimate format, unencumbered by criticism. Tracey's journals contain ideas, bits of inspiration, and unfinished art as well as comments and narratives.

I USUALLY KEEP A JOURNAL OF THIS SIZE AS WELL AS A SMALL ONE THAT FITS IN MY POCKET FOR WHEN I AM UNABLE TO BRING MY LARGER JOURNAL ALONG. THEY ARE WHAT KEEP ME SANE, AS I DUMP MY INSANITY INTO THEM. THEY OPEN A DOORWAY TO A PLACE WHERE I CAN PLAY, WRITE, SKETCH, AND EVEN SOCIALIZE WITH OTHERS, COMPLETELY WITHOUT RULES.

Artist: Tracy Moore

The Journal of Tracy Moore.
Artist: Tracy Moore

Step by Step:

ONE

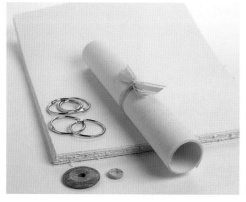

TWO

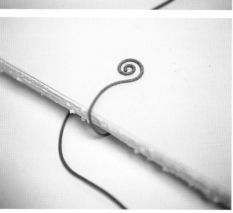

THREE

STEP ONE GATHER THE MATERIALS In this example, we will describe how to make a landscape-format book—one that is wider than it is tall—though your sketchbook can be any size you like. Be sure your pages are of uniform size and that your hole-punching tool can create holes in your pages large enough for the rings to fit through, but small enough so the rings don't slip, making the book unstable. You can find rings like the ones used here in local art- or craft-supply stores, or from the vendors listed in the back of the book.

STEP TWO CREATE THE COVER Be sure the hole punch can accommodate the cover material, which is thicker than the pages. In this example, we have chosen artists' canvas that is sturdy enough for our use. On the front cover, we have attached a large bead and coin to serve as a clasp to hold the book shut. Simply pre-punch small holes with an awl through the cover where you plan to place the clasp, and then sew the bead or coin in place with strong thread. On the back cover, a leather lace has been attached with copper thread. To close the book, wrap the lace around the coin.

STEP THREE PUNCH THE HOLES AND BIND THE BOOK When the covers are completed, punch or drill holes for the rings into the two covers and pages of the book at equal distances from the edges of the book. Then add the rings, tie the leather lace, and you're done!

So you're not an artist. You don't draw, paint, sketch, or even doodle well enough for a Post-it note. Have no fear. Your journals are an expression of your personal vision, private places to create as you see fit. Sometimes, it's hard not to feel intimidated when you see other artists' journals. Remember that your personal books are not finished artwork. They're not about the results as much as they are about process. Your journals are along for the journey, whether you're the next Da Vinci or, like the rest of us, you're not. Many projects discussed in this book that create beautiful results require little or no art background.

TOP: Katy Gilmore created this book at a gathering of people who keep illustrated field journals of daily writings. ABOVE: The cover of Elizabeth Steiner's sketchbook was inspired by the colors and shapes of Central Australia. ABOVE RIGHT: "Things to Do Until I See You Again" by Roz Stendahl discusses grief and the loss of mentors, and includes jottings attempting to answer the journal's title. FAR RIGHT: Roz Stendahl's sketchbooks primarily record nature-related items, but they have grown to include anything from a precise moment in time.

notes:

Take your sketchbook everywhere, so it will be at hand when inspiration hits.

Many reprinted artists' sketchbooks are available at your local bookstore or library. Take a look at what other artists have done with their sketchbooks for inspiration with yours.

When buying or creating a sketchbook, look for thicker paper, which can better tolerate artists' materials such as watercolor, inks, and oil or acrylic paints.

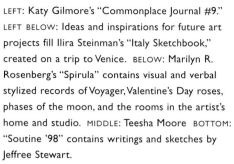

LEFT: Katy Gilmore's "Commonplace Journal #9." LEFT BELOW: Ideas and inspirations for future art projects fill Ilira Steinman's "Italy Sketchbook," created on a trip to Venice. BELOW: Marilyn R. Rosenberg's "Spirula" contains visual and verbal stylized records of Voyager, Valentine's Day roses, phases of the moon, and the rooms in the artist's home and studio. MIDDLE: Teesha Moore BOTTOM: "Soutine '98" contains writings and sketches by Jeffree Stewart.

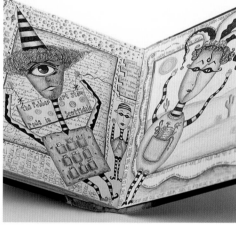

Triptychs and Books with Non-Linear Pages

MATERIALS

heavy stock paper for the cover

assorted drawing and printmaking papers

photographs

postcards

needle

bookbinding thread

binder's tape

glue

tape or other artists' materials to embellish the pages

Triptych is an ancient Greek word for early writing tablets that contained three hinged panels. In our examples, triptychs—also referred to as non-linear pages—are pages that fold outward from a journal in three parts. This technique is particularly useful for journals that aren't meant to be read from front to back. Artist Polly Smith has devised a creative binding to hold vacation mementos in her journal, "New Orleans Vacation Book." Her book has a front and back cover, but when it is opened, it reveals an unusual collection of different-size pages or leaves that can be read from left to right as well as right to left. The narrative can be read differently each time the book is opened, depending on how the reader turns the pages.

SINCE I DIDN'T HAVE TIME TO CONSTRUCT A BOOK BEFORE I LEFT ON VACATION, I BROUGHT LOOSE PAPER, PENCILS, AND WATERCOLORS WITH ME. I USED THESE MATERIALS TO CREATE THE PAGES, WHICH I LATER INDIVIDUALLY BOUND TO FLIP OPEN AND LIE FLAT.

Artist: Polly Smith

Step by Step:

ONE

TWO

STEP ONE **GATHER THE PAGES** Collect different-size sheets of heavy and durable artists' and printmaking papers. You may also create pages from photographs, post-cards, or other paper ephemera. The types of pages aren't as important as the collection as a whole. As the final book will contain pages of different sizes, the largest page in the group will dictate the final size of the book.

STEP TWO **SEW THE PAGES** Create one sewn edge on each sheet of paper in your non-linear book by sewing a blanket stitch on the binding side of your pages. The blanket stitching on each page must be of uniform distance apart, and the stitching must be wide enough for the binder's tape to slip underneath the thread.

notes:

Use different paper items for your pages such as ticket stubs, envelopes, packaging such as candy wrappers or wine labels, photographs, postcards, receipts, and paperback book covers.

The book in the step-by-step example has two sections. Try this technique with three, four, or more sections.

Add triptychs to your store-bought journals by tipping in folded pages with glue or sewing them into place with a needle and thread.

THREE

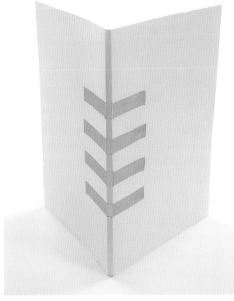

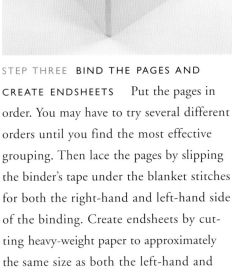

FOUR

What are your dreams? Not the ones you have when you're asleep, but your desires for yourself, your family, and your future? Write down who it is you want to be, who you wish you were, your successes, and your failures. Write about your joys and personal achievements. Your journal is a quiet place where you can say what doesn't get said in everyday life. Be as honest as you can. If it's hard to open up in your daily journal, create a private one. You are who you are, and an honest journal will be more important to you in years to come than a censored one.

STEP THREE **BIND THE PAGES AND CREATE ENDSHEETS**   Put the pages in order. You may have to try several different orders until you find the most effective grouping. Then lace the pages by slipping the binder's tape under the blanket stitches for both the right-hand and left-hand side of the binding. Create endsheets by cutting heavy-weight paper to approximately the same size as both the left-hand and right-hand side of the binding. Glue the stray ends of the binder's tape onto the backside of the endsheets.

STEP FOUR **CREATE THE COVER AND ASSEMBLE THE BOOK**   The cover of your book will not only hold all the pages, but will also hide the endsheets holding the pages together. The final cover should be at least half an inch larger than the pages, so as to comfortably accommodate the endsheets. Start with a sheet of heavy stock that is as tall as the final book, but three times as wide. First, fold the cover in half. Then fold the right and left sides of the cover inward to create the pockets to slip the endsheets into. Polly Smith has sewn the folds together at the top and bottom of her book so the endsheets won't slip out when the book is read, but glue will also work. When the pockets for the endsheets are created, slip the left and right endsheets into these pockets, and you've created your non-linear book. Embellish the book cover as appropriate.

LEFT: The structure of Elizabeth Clark's accordion-fold book is analogous to the way memories tend to naturally evolve. BELOW: Juliana Cole's "Guidebook for the Distant Traveler." FACING PAGE: "Mapping Mission Creek" commemorates a place behind Roberta Lavadour's home, and includes a map that visually speaks of experience and memory.

MAPPING
MISSION
CREEK

Mixed Media
Roberta Lavadour
1999

Created in an
edition of 10
of which this is
8 of 10

Nature Journals

MATERIALS

fresh leaves or flowers

spray glass cleaner

inks or watercolors

paper towels

Garden journals are books that record the progress in and experiences from planting and tending gardens. One element commonly found in garden journals is leaf and flower impressions. Adding the inked impressions of favorite plants onto journal pages is a fun way to illustrate gardening successes and memories. Betty Auchard has kept leaf-impression journals for over ten years. Her journals contain plant impressions from her home in California as well as from travels throughout the United States and Canada. The technique is very simple and straightforward, and can be mastered in an afternoon. This process can also be used in daily journals to visually record places, events, or outdoor experiences.

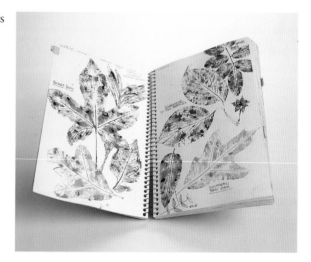

MY SKETCHBOOKS VISUALLY RECORD MY TRAVELS THROUGHOUT NORTH AMERICA——NOT WITH PHOTOGRAPHS, BUT INSTEAD WITH COLLECTIONS OF PLANT AND LEAF IMPRESSIONS FROM THE PLACES I HAVE VISITED.

Artist: Betty Auchard

Step by Step:

ONE

TWO

THREE

STEP ONE **PREPARE THE LEAF** Begin with a fresh, dry leaf or flower. Spray the vein side of the leaf with glass cleaner to remove the natural oils that many plants contain, which may make the leaf resistant to inks or watercolors. Blot the leaf dry before continuing.

STEP TWO **PAINT THE LEAF** Apply ink to the vein side of the leaf. Place the leaf on your journal page, paint-side down, and carefully and gently cover with a paper towel, which will serve as a presser sheet as well as a blotter to soak up extra ink.

STEP THREE **PRINT THE LEAF** Press, don't rub, every part of the leaf surface. Carefully remove the paper towel and leaf to reveal the transferred image.

notes:

If you apply too much water or paint to the leaf, the final impression may smear.

Be sure to cover the entire leaf with pigment, even painting beyond the edges of the leaf. If any part of the leaf is not painted, it won't be printed.

While pressing the print by hand, hold the leaf in place with a finger at all times to keep the print from smearing.

Many books on journal-keeping that describe how and what to write can be found in your local bookstores. If you're creating a journal specifically to document your personal history, you may find these types of books inspirational. Many contain prompts to get the creative juices flowing. Try creating your own personal prompts such as the ones listed below. Keep your list somewhere in your journal to get you motivated when you find yourself staring at the blank page.

Once again, I don't know what to write. The last time this happened I ...

This is who I am today ...

This is what I did today ...

This is what I like best / least about this (journal, pen, day, place, house, life, body) ...

I keep journals because ...

I wish I was ... / I'm glad I'm not ...

If I could write in my journal to anyone it would be ...

The next artistic technique I'm going to attempt in my journal is ...

The best thing about my journal is ...

ABOVE LEFT: Betty Auchard's sketchbooks visually record her travels throughout North America without photographs, but instead with collections of plant and leaf impressions from the places she has visited. ABOVE RIGHT: Lori Kay Ludwig created this book to record the change of seasons, experienced during daily walks, following a recent relocation. TOP: Using a very simple technique, Betty Auchard's leaf transfer journals contain richly varied looks at the fauna gathered from her travels throughout North America.

TOP LEFT: Roz Stendahl keeps sketchbooks and journals to note nature-related items, but they have grown to include anything and everything from a single precise moment. LEFT AND FACING PAGE: Peter Madden made this book over a month one spring while he was cleaning out his garden. He found thumbnail-size remnants of leaves from the previous summer and incorporated them into this piece. BELOW: After a move, Lori Kay Ludwig created this book, which she calls "Transplant," to record the change of the seasons as she experienced them during her daily walks.

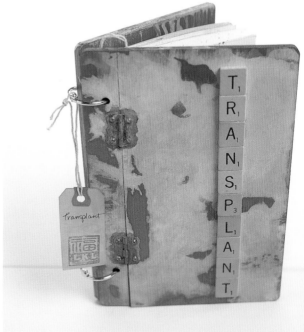

Journal Techniques

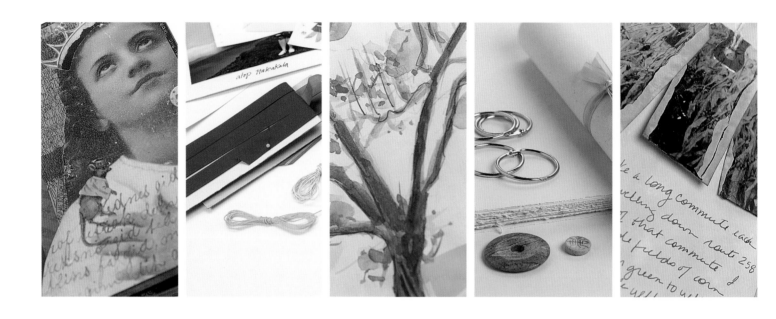

Advanced journal techniques such as those found in the following chapters can help make your journal something special. Projects such as image transfers and one-of-a-kind carved stamps will help you design visually stunning pages.

The books you create should reflect your personal vision and esthetic sense, whether that be funky or arty, crafty or flowery. Like different painters using the same paints, these techniques can be utilized to create many different looks and designs, and they can be used by those of us just learning to be artistic and seasoned journalers alike. And if something doesn't work out right the first time, you can always turn the page and start again.

Wax Resist

MATERIALS

wax-based crayon or other wax source such as a candle

paint brush

water-based inks or watercolors

Wax resist is a simple and attractive technique for adding visual flair to journal pages. The materials are probably in your home or studio already, and the effect can be utilized in journals with many different themes. In the examples on these pages, artist Ilira Steinman uses wax resist as headings and sometimes complete pages for her yoga journal. The imprecise and ethereal effects resulting from the combination of wax and inks complements nicely the imagery and text of her writings.

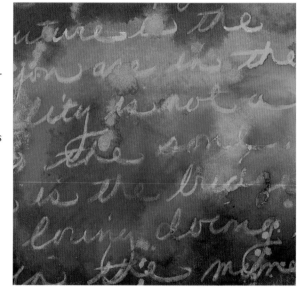

I USE MY JOURNAL AS A WAY TO RECORD MEMORABLE EXPERIENCES FROM MY WEEKLY YOGA CLASSES AS WELL AS SPECIAL SEMINARS WITH VISITING TEACHERS. SOMETIMES, I RECORD MY THOUGHTS IN A SMALL NOTEBOOK AND THEN TRANSLATE THE WRITINGS INTO VISUAL IMAGERY IN MY JOURNAL.

Artist: Ilira Steinman

Ilira Steinman created this book as a way to transcribe the inspiration she gains during her Yoga practice.

Step by Step:

ONE

TWO

THREE

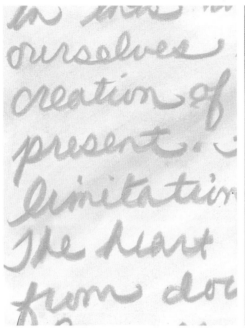

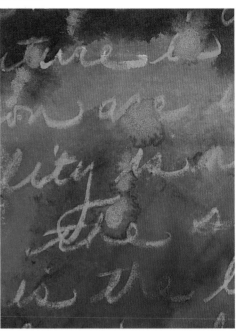

STEP ONE **CREATE WITH WAX** In this example, a wax crayon was used to create the text. Note that contrasting colors between the text and background work best.

STEP TWO **START THE WASH** Before you begin to add colored ink over and around the wax base, wet the area to allow the ink to saturate the page completely.

STEP THREE **ADD AN INK WASH OVER THE WAX BASE** Next, add a contrasting ink color over the wax base. Remove any pools of ink on top of the wax with a cotton swab or tissue paper, and allow the page to dry.

Some people find that their best journal writing happens when they let their minds wander and forget about punctuation, grammar and spelling. When they do not see a beginning and end to an entry before they start to write, they find they are more intuitive and honest. It is one of the reasons why many journalers feel travel journals contain some of the most creative writings — our minds are full of new experiences, so we're not under pressure to decide what to write about. And at the same time, we feel compelled to write as much as possible while we're away on a travel adventure.

Paradoxically, some writers are also at their most creative when they are under pressure, perhaps because they have a specific purpose for creating in their journals. For instance, they might want to create something unique because they'll soon be seeing a friend whose journals they envy, or they might be trying to create a few outstanding first pages in their journals.

Fill your journal with a rich array of pictures as well as words. Use the wax resist technique to add colorful headings and even full-page art to journal pages. The artist Wendy Hale Davis created vivid illustrations and decorative type in wax resist to blend with her journal writing.

notes:

Different types of wax will work nicely for this technique, including beeswax, bookbinder's wax (used to coat thread), and especially crayons.

Use contrasting colors to make a more pronounced resist effect.

The effect can also be used to create backgrounds, borders, and complete pages.

Blender Pen

MATERIALS

a blender pen containing xylene

binder clips

copy machine (black and white or color)

bone folder

An extremely easy, flexible, and creative visual journal-keeping technique is the use of a blender pen to transfer simple images and printed text from black and white or color copies onto journal pages. Simply write out your text on your computer using an interesting font, photocopy it in reverse by using the mirror-image option, and then use a blender pen to transfer the printed text onto your journal page. You can then add color or other-wise enhance the image to create the look you desire.

I CREATED THIS DAILY JOURNAL TO BE A VESSEL FOR EVERYDAY IDEAS, FROM THE MUNDANE TO THE NOTEWORTHY.

Artist: Jason Thompson

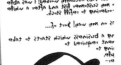

Step by Step:

USING A BLENDER PEN TO TRANSFER TEXT

ONE

TWO

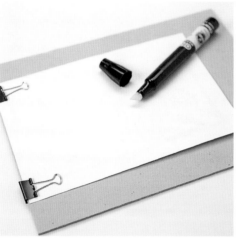

THREE

STEP ONE **PRINT OR COPY IN REVERSE**
Either print a master sheet in reverse and photocopy it, or use the mirror-image option on a copy machine to create a backwards image. (**Note:** Only the output from a copy machine will work because this process requires toner.)

STEP TWO **USE THE BLENDER PEN**
Use binder clips to attach the photocopy to your journal. Any movement of the photocopy will result in a blurred transfer. Liberally wipe the blender pen across the back of the photocopy, and press firmly against the journal page with a bone folder or other burnishing tool—you can sometimes use the back end of the blender pen if you don't have a bone folder available. Work in small areas no larger than the size of a silver dollar at a time. Allow the chemicals in the blender pen to fully saturate the photocopy.

STEP THREE **REMOVE THE MASTER IMAGE AND ALLOW TO DRY** Carefully peel back the photocopy to reveal the transfer. You may need to repeat the process on areas that haven't been transferred completely. (**Note:** This process will not completely remove all of the toner from your photocopy.)

Try writing from a third-person point of view. Replace "I" with "he" or "she." Write about an experience as if you were someone else, someone watching from the outside. The distance may make discussing something difficult a little easier. Try writing in your journal as if you're writing a letter. Write this letter to a friend, to the future, maybe even to the future you! Write both points of view of a topic. For instance, if you find yourself expressing negative feelings or thoughts, pretend these thoughts are part of a conversation and take another person's side, someone with a different point of view.

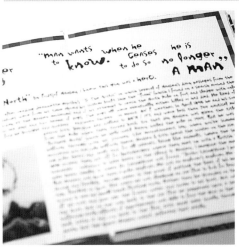

notes:

Always use a blender pen in a well-ventilated area, either inside with a fan on and the windows open, or outdoors. Read and follow all manufacturers' warnings before using any solvent.

Use your computer to lay out text onto a page the same size as your journal and transfer the entire printed page into your book.

If you only have one copy of your favorite photo or newspaper article, make a color photocopy of it and use the blender pen to transfer it into your journal.

Image Transfers

MATERIALS

xylene solvent

bone folder

can with a lid

rags

respirator, face mask, or fan

binder clips

Note: The chemicals used in these steps can be toxic. Read all manufacturer's safety precautions before attempting these techniques.

Though the process is essentially the same as using a blender pen, using solvents to transfer images from photocopies is more involved, allows better control over the transfer, and results in a more distinct image that is less wispy. Artist Lori Kay Ludwig uses solvents to render photographs more intimate. This technique allows the repeated use of images without the need for a darkroom and permits her to be more involved with the image than a traditional photograph might.

I CREATED THIS BOOK TO RECORD MY TRANSITION TO MOTHERHOOD. IT CONTAINS IMPORTANT VISUAL RECORDS OF MY PERSONAL AND EMOTIONAL DEVELOPMENT.

Artist: Lori Kay Ludwig

6 MONTHS

Changing faster now...
Skin is luminous, rosy
even my FACE has gained
weight
Stronger, though my belly
is bigger every morning
hard to cat after a meal?

Baby do to my life?
m disappear? Will
at about

SEVEN
MONTHS

Step by Step:

USING SOLVENTS TO TRANSFER IMAGES

ONE

TWO

THREE

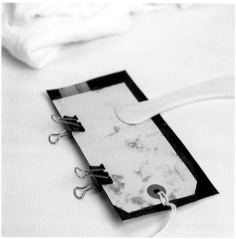
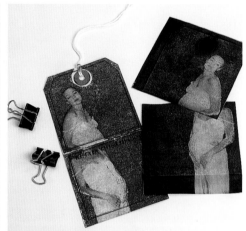

STEP ONE **PREPARE YOUR SUPPLIES** Pour about two inches of xylene into a can with a lid. Make sure your rags and burnishing tool are handy. Wear rubber gloves and a respirator, and use a fan in a well-ventilated area, or work outside. Place your photo-copied image face-down onto the page and clip into place with binder clips.

STEP ONE **APPLY THE SOLVENT** Dip the rag into the can. The rag should be thoroughly wet but not dripping. Rub the solvent onto the backside of your photo-copy, covering a small section of the image at a time. Burnish each section as you go with your burnishing tool. Take a peek every so often to see which areas need to be burnished again. Don't be surprised if you need to apply solvent to or burnish an area a few times before you achieve the desired effect.

STEP THREE **REMOVE THE PHOTO-COPY** Remove the binder clips and peel away the photocopy. In some places, the toner may have adhered the paper, leaving tiny, thin, threadlike bits on the image when the pho-tocopy is peeled back. This is considered an advantage, as it lends a hand-drawn appear-ance to your final image. You can now enhance the image with colored pencils, charcoal, pastel, watercolor—whatever works best with your own journal.

Some journals are kept in chronological order, starting on the first page and ending on the last page, while some have entries arbitrarily entered throughout the book. If you're intimidated by the first blank page in a book, try creating your first entry somewhere in the middle of the book, or start your journal the same way every time. For example, you might always begin your journal with a page describing who you are, where you are, and how you obtained or made the book: what fabric you used, how long it took to bind, where you made it. You might also write about the last journal you kept, how much time it spanned, and what you liked about it. After you've made the first entry, you'll feel less apprehensive about the prospect of all those blank pages.

The images in this book were found vacation photos discovered in antique shops. All the images show cobble-stones in them. Artist: Roberta Lavadour

notes:

Always use solvents such as xylene in a well-ventilated area, either inside with a fan on and the windows open, or outdoors.

Other solvents besides xylene will work to transfer images, and can also produce results of a different opacity and hue. Try this technique using acetone, lighter fluid, hairspray, peppermint oil, or denatured alcohol.

Try adding transfer images from a special trip into a travel journal, baby pictures into a new baby journal, or pictures of friends and family into a daily journal to document the people in your life.

Sewing and Non-Adhesive Inclusions

MATERIALS

needle, thread or other sewing material

scissors

When we want to attach items onto journal pages, the first thing that comes to mind is glue. Adhesives are transparent; they're the medium, not part of the composition. Sewing, however, is part of the composition. To include more texture to journal pages, artist Peter Madden decoratively sews meaningful objects into his journals and artist books. In his journal, "Relic," Peter has collected items from his past, his family, and places he's visited, and catalogued them into book form. The technique is very straightforward, and sewing experience is not necessary. Furthermore, as sewing showcases the thread, you can use the thread as a decorative element.

THIS SCRAPBOOK, CALLED "RELIQUIAE II," IS A MEANS OF PRESERVING AND DESCRIBING A COLLECTION OF PERSONAL ESOTERICA.

Artist: Peter Madden

ABOVE: Peter Madden's "Reliquiae II"

rel·ic (rel′ik) n. [ME. relike < OFr. relique < L. reliquiae, pl., remains] 1. a) an object, custom, etc. that has survived, wholly or partially from the past b) something that has historical interest because of its age and associations with the past, or that serves as a keepsake, or souvenir 2. [pl.] remaining fragments; surviving parts; ruins.

Step by Step:

ONE	TWO	THREE

STEP ONE **SEW AROUND ORGANIC MATERIALS**   In this example, Peter has sewn rose stems into his book. Note how the thread creates a unique pattern along the stems.

STEP TWO **SEW IN A POCKET**   The thread in this example not only creates a pattern along the edge of the lace that forms a pocket, but also follows the theme of the needle and thread underneath the lace.

STEP THREE **SEW IN EPHEMERA**   The simple technique of sewing in paper ephemera adds dimension to these otherwise visually simple elements. Note also that in the three examples here, the pages of Peter's books are themselves sewn together. This is not only a design element but also allows the ends of the threads to be hidden between the pages.

notes:

Try sewing with thread, twine, wire, raffia, plastic ties, yarn, embroidery floss, string, or ribbon.

If you're concerned about the stray ends of the thread, let both ends terminate underneath the page you're working on, and secure and hide the trailing ends on the backside with tape or a collage or some other visual element.

To create neatly executed sewn patterns, mark your journal page with a template before actually piercing the page with the needle.

Where do you write? Do you write all the time? Only at set times and only in certain places? If it helps to inspire you, try setting aside either a place or a time to write and create on a regular basis. Maybe you write before you go to bed, or you have a small studio with your art supplies. Perhaps you find yourself inspired to create at random moments during the day. If so, keep your journal with you at all times. Write during your morning coffee, on the train to work, during lunch, at school, after work, or at home alone. Creating a special place where you feel comfortable can be inspiration enough to get your journal and journaling supplies together.

ABOVE: This is the original book of artists Judy and Mallory Serebrin's collaborative series. RIGHT: This collaborative book is the second in a series that began as a birthday present from Mallory Serebrin to her sister Judy. Both women are artists and send the book back and forth to help them stay connected.

TOP AND LEFT: Judy Serebrin's daily journal traveled with her from Seattle to Israel. BELOW: Peter Madden's journals embody themes of memory and loss. BELOW LEFT: Peter Madden's hand-bound book with hammered copper on wood covers has mixed-media pages with computer-generated text. FACING PAGE TOP: "Memories Revisited" by Maria Pisano commemorates the daily life of the artist's parents, capturing moments that were not necessarily highlights, but celebrated who they were. FACING PAGE BELOW: This book, called "Big Book III," is very different from the others Juliana Coles has created. She works in this book with her students during classes.

Paper Cutting

MATERIALS

matte knife

ruler

cutting mat

pencil

eraser

The idea of making cuts in journal pages to allow photographs to be added to them came simply from wanting to place a photograph onto a page of a journal and not having either a glue stick, photo-corners, or tape available. It quickly became apparent, however, that this creative technique can be used to add visual interest to journal pages even if the option of using glue or photocorners is available. The concept is straightforward, and yet there are limitless creative combinations. The technique is particularly great to use in a travel journal. On these pages, you'll find a few examples of cut pages with photographs as well as other objects inserted into journals using the same technique.

WHILE SEARCHING FOR A LOFT IN PROVIDENCE, RHODE ISLAND, I CREATED THIS BOOK AS A PLACE TO STORE INFORMATION SUCH AS ADDRESSES, REALTORS' NUMBERS, AND PICTURES OF BUILDINGS.

Artist: Jason Thompson

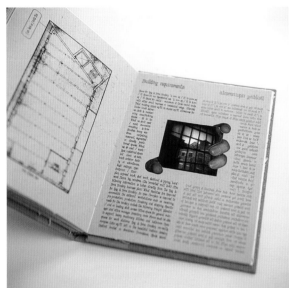

Step by Step:

PAPER CUTTING

ONE

TWO

THREE

STEP ONE CREATE THE BACKGROUND
In this example, a black and white image of a hand holding a picture will form the frame around the photograph that is to be inserted into the journal. Once cut, the fingers will serve as photocorners, holding the photograph in place.

STEP TWO CUT THE BACKGROUND
Outline the photograph with a pencil to form the edges that will be cut out of the page. Next, cut around all of the portions of the black and white image that will show over the photograph.

STEP THREE PLACE THE PHOTOGRAPH
Erase any pencil marks that may show around the finished layout. Slip the photograph into the slots formed by the cuts.

After looking through so many journals created by different artists and journalers, we've discovered some common elements among them that you may find in your own journals.

INSPIRATION Many journalers sew or glue items of inspiration into their journals such as images from other journaler's books, postcards from gallery and art exhibits, pictures from magazines, photographs, or inspirational quotes and writings.

PICTURES OF PETS Somehow cat and dog pictures always make it into our journals.

COFFEE RINGS It's almost a requirement to have a coffee-cup ring in your journal.

HAPPY AND SAD Journalers often find their deepest inspiration when writing about tragedies and triumphs.

FIRST PERSON Who do you write to? Many journalers like to write to themselves.

THIS BOOK BELONGS TO: Don't forget this one. I once left my journal in a rental truck, and the next person who rented the truck called me to say they had found it!

ABOVE AND RIGHT: Roberta Lavadour created this book to commemorate a place along a creek behind her home. The book contains a map, which visually speaks of experience and memory instead of geography.

notes:

To permanently use cutout pages to showcase photographs in your journal, place a bit of glue or double-sided tape to the back of larger photographs.

Cut corners don't have to be used to hold photographs. Try using them to add flowers, feathers, currency, stamps, or other ephemera to your journal.

Remember that the other side of your page will show portions of your photograph poking through. To hide these corners, paste a collage or something special on the page.

More Than Handwriting

MATERIALS

newspaper or magazines

scissors

rubber stamps

pens

pencils

paints

brushes

Artist Maura Cluthe creates beautiful, simple, everyday journals utilizing many visual elements, including text-based entries that contain more than handwriting. She adds words to her journals using techniques that include copying and pasting typed entries and using rubber-stamp alphabets. These techniques give more weight to the words she uses by making them more visual. Pictures alone may also convey dialogue, just as words can be used to create visual elements, as seen in the examples here.

I CARRY SKETCHBOOKS WITH ME TO RECORD WHAT I

SEE AS A STARTING POINT FOR LARGER WORKS.

Artist: Maura Cluthe

Artist: Maura Cluthe

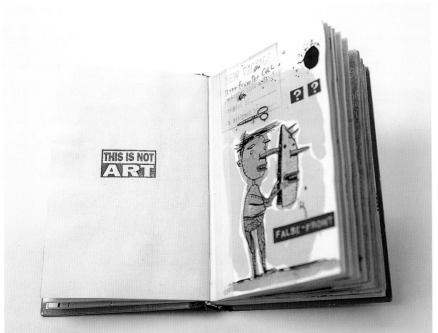

Step by Step:

ONE

TWO

This book contains ideas and inspiration for larger works of art. It's one of the sketchbooks Maura Cluthe says she carries with her everywhere.

THREE

STEP ONE **USE RUBBER STAMPS**
Though it takes more time, using a rubber-stamp alphabet is a distinct way to add words to your journal pages. Try using different sets of stamps or different-colored stamp pads.

STEP TWO **CUT AND PASTE** Try cutting and pasting text printed from a computer. Use unusual fonts, move the text around the page, and explore different sizes and colors for the words.

STEP THREE **SAY IT LOUD!** Different-size text entries can convey different volumes of speech, just as in real life. The bigger, the louder; the smaller, the quieter. Use text that complements what you're trying to say.

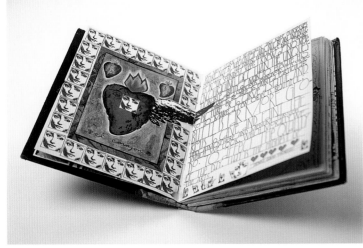

These journals are from Teesha Moore's Everyday Journal series. TOP AND RIGHT: "Everyday Journal #3." ABOVE: "Everyday Journal #1."

A definite vision will help inspire you when you don't feel like creating. Think of how you would answer if a friend asked you why you keep a journal. Do you keep it for the memories? For the art? Because it's inspirational or therapeutic? Maybe you find yourself drawn to journals and don't know why. Perhaps you saw someone else's books and were inspired to keep your own. Think about what your reasons are and write them down in every journal you create. Revisit your answers when you find yourself with creator's block.

notes:

If you're bored with writing entries in your journals from left to right, try writing sideways, upside-down, along the gutter, or across the entire two-page spread.

Mix things up by using different techniques to add words to a page, allowing the words themselves to become visual elements.

Try using dymo tape; cutouts from newspapers and magazines; and even copies of Web sites, computer images, or the handwriting of your friends and family.

Plaster Paper

MATERIALS

dry stretched paper

spackle

spackle knife

sandpaper

dust mask

texturing tools

acrylic paint

wax

spray-mount adhesive

Surface treatments give journal pages an extra layered element and visual interest. One of the most unusual surface treatments is Melissa Slattery's plaster paper technique. This unique process creates a distressed and "shabby chic" look. This technique lends itself well to pages that contain minimal text entries or to travel journals with specific color schemes. For instance, a visit to Sienna, Italy, may inspire you to create journal pages with sienna hues to them. Rich colors also look fabulous. Try this technique out for yourself and see what types of creative entries it inspires.

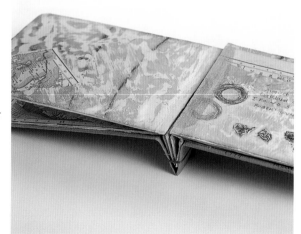

THIS BOOK CONTAINS PAGES CREATED WITH MY PLASTER PAPER TECHNIQUE. IT IS A TRAVEL JOURNAL OF SORTS, WITH ARTWORK CREATED WITH PASTEL, GRAPHITE, AND COLLAGE, AMONG OTHER TECHNIQUES.

Artist: Melissa Slattery

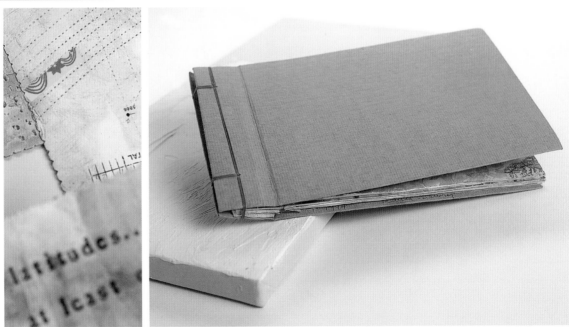

Artist: Mellissa Slattery

Step by Step:

ONE	TWO	THREE

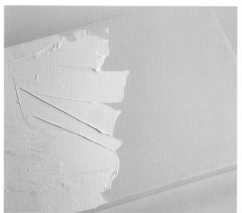 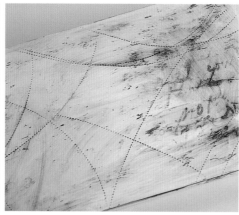 

STEP ONE **APPLY THE SPACKLE** Either stretch the paper you wish to work on or, if you are working directly in a journal, use a spray-mount adhesive to temporarily attach a backer such as Davey board, a bookbinder's board used to create hardcovers, to the under-side of your page to prevent warping. Before working directly in your journal, however, you might wish to practice this technique on a piece of scrap paper first. Apply a thin layer of spackle with a putty knife, making sure not to apply too much.

STEP TWO **SAND AND CREATE TEXTURE** Lightly sand the surface with a fine-grade sandpaper to smooth away any deep grooves. To add texture to your page, create patterns on or distress the spackle as it is drying. Allow the spackle to dry before continuing. Once the plaster is sanded and dry, you can begin to add color to the surface with acrylic paint, watercolors, inks, shoe polish, or graphite.

STEP THREE **FINALIZE THE DESIGN** Once color has been added, you can rubber-stamp, collage, paint, or even incise the surface with linoleum or wood-block cutting tools to create the look you desire.

notes:

Because this process creates thick pages, use this technique in an expandable journal with heavy pages, or bind your own book with the pages after they've been created.

Try adding a liberal amount of beeswax to "crayonize" the surface. Remove excess beeswax with a spatula, and polish with a soft cloth.

Cover any collaged images with a matte-finish, clear-coat spray enamel and allow to dry.

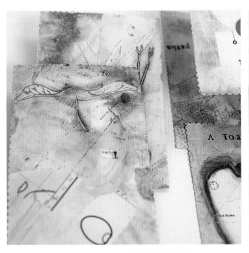

You don't have to keep a journal faithfully. Some people keep journals on and off during their lives, sometmes going years without writing. There are times in life when you might not need to keep a journal, so do your best not to feel guilty when you're not writing or creating in one. Time will pass, and then one day you will find an old journal (or maybe it will find you), and the process begins again. There will always be a blank book waiting for us at any given time in our lives. Journal keeping shouldn't be a chore, it should be a release. Think of your journals as friends who are always there for you, not simply as appointments that must be kept.

Created with Mellissa Slattery's plaster paper technique, these artistic 'cards' are enclosed in a wax paper folder and tied with measuring tape ribbon.

Emulsion Lifts

MATERIALS

camera that uses pack film

pack film

candy thermometer

tea kettle

glass or Pyrex trays to hold water

contact or shelf paper

scissors

wax paper

clear-coat spray enamel

brayer or bone folder

An exciting and advanced technique for adding photographic imagery to your journals is a process called an emulsion lift. This involved process requires lifting or removing the very delicate emulsion from photograph paper and then adhering it to your journal pages. One of the nice results of this technique is that the transferred emulsion is so thin that you can barely feel that it's there, but the image remains vivid and crisp. Lori Kay Ludwig uses emulsion lifts extensively in her journals. In the example here, she has utilized an altered book to create a journal documenting the changing of the seasons which contains emulsion lifts almost exclusively, even on the cover.

I CREATED THIS ONE-OF-A-KIND ARTISTS' BOOK TO RECORD THE MONTH OF OCTOBER 1999.

Artist: Lori Kay Ludwig

BELOW: This is a solvent transfer. BOTTOM: This emulsion-lift monthly journal is a hand-bound, recycled arithmetic book from 1852.

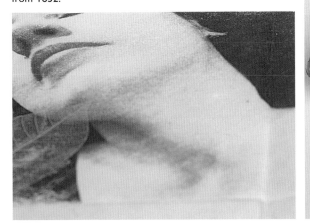

Step by Step:

EMULSION LIFTS

ONE

TWO

STEP ONE **HEAT THE WATER** Note that this process only works with cameras that use pack film, a special film by Polaroid that is the only type of film that works with this technique. Ask your local camera shop for more information regarding cameras that use this type of film. Pour a tea kettle's worth of water that is exactly 160 degrees Fahrenheit (71 degrees Celsius) into the tray. Carefully monitor the water's temperature with the thermometer. Adhere contact or shelf paper to the back of the photograph to prevent the backing of the print from dissolving in the water.

STEP TWO **IMMERSE THE PHOTO-GRAPH IN WATER** Submerge your photograph in the water for approximately four minutes. During this time, you should start to see bubbles form underneath the image, and the edges will start to loosen. Gently rock the tray if necessary to hasten the process.

Creating lists is a way to keep a personal inventory of who and where we are at any given moment. Try creating a list of who you are at different times in your life. For example, I am a husband, artist, diarist, computer user, mediator, son, writer, webmaster, cat lover, boss, employer, bookbinder, and friend. See how these lists change as you enter different phases in your life. Look back on them and see if the person you were years ago is the same as the person you are now.

THREE

FOUR

STEP THREE **REMOVE THE EMULSION**
When the emulsion starts to peel away from the photograph, carefully float the emulsion on top of a clean sheet of wax paper and flatten any wrinkles or creases. Next, carefully remove the wax paper and the emulsion from the water.

STEP FOUR **PLACE THE EMULSION INTO YOUR JOURNAL** Carefully lift the thin layer of emulsion off the wax paper and place it onto your journal page. It may crease, crinkle, or even tear. Be prepared to accept these effects as part of your composition. Press the image lightly with a brayer to remove any water or air bubbles from beneath its surface and seal with a spray enamel.

notes:

This process creates very vivid and clear images in such an unusual way that you should consider using the images for special pages or even the cover of your journal.

Try playing around with the way the emulsion crinkles and folds as it is transferred.

The ethereal effect of emulsion-lift transfers looks great in dream journals!

Carved Stamps

MATERIALS

**large eraser or
wine cork**

**carving tools such
as linoleum or
wood-carving knives**

ink

Although a few early entrepreneurs have claimed
the title, no one knows who created the first rubber stamp. Suffice it to say, today's rubber stamps
have come a long way from those created to ease
the printing bills of manufacturers in the 1800s.
Artist Teesha Moore not only uses many rubber
stamps in her journals but even sells her own line
of stamps to other journalers and artists. The
stamps she creates are unique and showcase her
own particular vision. We will show you how to
create your very own one-of-a-kind, custom-made
eraser and cork stamps.

THESE ARE MY CREATIVE PLAYGROUND JOURNALS. AS FAR
AS A THEME GOES, THE QUOTE, "ART AND LIFE ARE ONE,"
COMES TO MIND. I DO WHAT I FEEL LIKE ON THE PAGES
FOR THAT PARTICULAR DAY WITH NO RULES.

Artist: Teesha Moore

Teesha Moore's hand-stamped art journals include Everyday Journals #1 and #3.

Step by Step:

ONE

TWO

STEP ONE ERASER STAMPS: DRAW YOUR
OUTLINE   Draw an outline of the image
you wish to cut on the eraser. Try simple
forms to begin with. If you're a better writer
than artist, you can use a blender pen to
transfer computer-generated text or images
onto the surface of the stamp. Remember
that the image on the stamp must be carved
in reverse! Using a small, sharp blade, carefully carve away the eraser around your
image. Cut outward from your image to
avoid undercutting your stamp.

STEP TWO   PRINT! When you've finished
carving, practice stamping a few times and
remove any unwanted portions of the eraser that are visible when stamped. The print
from a cork stamp leaves a more distressed
impression, which creates an artful effect.

notes:

Paint different-colored inks onto single
stamps for a more colorful effect.

To create stamps with two or more
colors, carve identical stamps with
different portions removed. Print the
first stamp in one color, and the second in another, carefully lining up
the stamps when you print.

Create a set of alphabet or number
stamps out of cork for making headings,
dates, and page numbers in your
journals.

ONE

TWO

STEP ONE **CORK STAMPS: DRAW YOUR OUTLINE** To create interesting, carved wine corks, begin with a cork that has a flat surface. If the surface of the cork isn't flat, it won't print correctly. If necessary, you can use a sharp blade to slice off the top or bottom of a cork prior to carving. Draw the image you wish to carve on the cork. Cutting cork is harder than carving an eraser. Be sure to use a sharp blade, and handle it carefully when you are cutting.

STEP TWO **PRINT!**

If you have concerns about creating a perfect journal, or if you find the blank page intimidating, spread your ideas out by keeping a diary, a journal, and a sketchbook simultaneously. Your diary may contain mostly written entries, and you should write in it regularly. Your journal can be a place to experiment with different artistic techniques like the ones taught in this book. And your sketchbook can be a place for you to flesh out ideas for other artistic works such as paintings or illustrations.

FACING PAGE: Teesha Moore's Everyday Journal #1
ABOVE: Peter Madden's tray of cork stamps. LEFT AND
BOTTOM: Teesha Moore's Everyday Journal #1

Journals as Art

MATERIALS

water color

inks

tape

glue

acrylic paint

gesso

crayons

colored pencils, etc.

For some journalers, when the creative process fully opens up and they begin to completely express themselves in their journals, their books become works of art. This is especially the case with the journals of Juliana Coles, which contain thoughts and dreams from her daily life. Though the visual and written elements in her books are confessional, reading them isn't voyeuristic; she simply wants to share herself with others, and her journals are the medium. In these examples, we can see how a personal journal, though essentially private, can be created with the knowledge that it will be shared with others, and should rightfully be considered a work of art.

THIS BOOK IS VERY DIFFERENT FROM THE OTHERS I HAVE CREATED. I WORK IN THIS BOOK WITH MY STUDENTS DURING CLASSES. IN IT I DON'T FEEL CONSTRAINED TO BE AN ARTIST. IT'S MORE PLAYFUL, LESS HEAVY.

Artist: Juliana Coles

ABOVE AND LEFT: Juliana Coles' journal began as an artist sketchbook, which over time turned into a visual journal containing self portraits, dreams, ideas for project and poems.

Step by Step:

ONE

TWO

THREE

STEP ONE **SKETCH YOURSELF IN A SELF-PORTRAIT**   Self portraits are extremely personal and revealing, saying a great deal about a person and their state of mind. Self-portraits from different periods of your life can reveal different messages that you may only fully understand after the passage of time.

STEP TWO **SAY WHAT YOU FEEL**   If you expect others to read your journals, you may be more inclined to say and write what you might otherwise consider obvious. Words of wisdom, which may ordinarily be scattered throughout your journal entries, can become entire pages supported by appropriate visual elements. You are special in your own way and have your own vision—share it with the world.

STEP THREE **RETELL YOUR STORIES**   The stories and experiences from your own life can be written in a manner other than a first-person narrative. For instance, Juliana Coles expressed her narratives in visual form. Some of these pages contain graphic novel–type panels, and others are written in unusual scripts that convey more than just what the words say—the colors, the images, and the layout all help to further express her thoughts.

notes:

Can't draw? Try collage or using rubberstamps, or create images on a computer and use a blender pen or solvents to transfer them onto your journal pages. Use these images as a basis for creative entries.

Creating an entry without words is a great way to visualize your own thoughts. You may be surprised by the outcome.

Try working in a medium you're not familiar with. Take pictures if you're not a photographer, for example, or try your hand at watercolors if you haven't done so before.

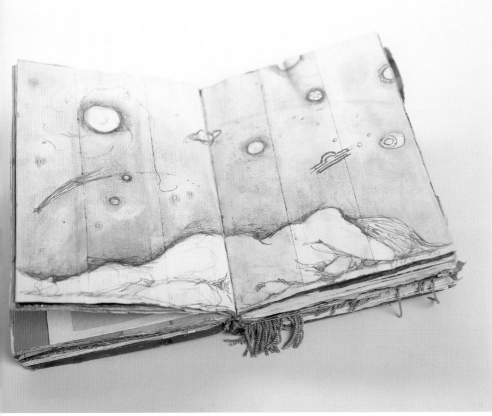

A fine pen and a blank journal make a wonderful gift for a child. Show your own journal to others, and maybe you will inspire them to start keeping a journal, too. Here are a few suggestions for giving a blank book to a friend or family member:

HAND-BOUND BLANK BOOK Make one yourself if you can.

PEN AND INK Fountain pens along with a bottle of ink make great gifts.

JOURNAL SUPPLIES Colored pencils, a glue stick, photocorners, watercolors, a paint brush, and other artists' supplies will help inspire different ways of using a journal. Look through the materials list chapter for more inspiration.

JOURNAL BOX Put all of these items into a portable box, such as an artist's wooden paint box, or even decorate a small carrying case.

ABOVE: Juliana Coles used this book as a creative journal to follow along with writer Julia Cameron's *The Artist's Way* exercises. ABOVE LEFT: Juliana created this book to contain less serious artwork. It is a playful journal with many items attached to the pages.

Thinking Outside the Book

Webster's American English dictionary defines the word book as "a set of written, printed, or blank sheets bound together into a volume." Though we generally picture "bound" as including two covers and a spine, there are many ways to bind together sheets to form a volume. In fact, as seen in the examples here, collecting or assembling our thoughts or daily writings together does not require the use of a traditional book. The examples by Roz Stendahl and Ilira Steinman demonstrate that a box can hold entries. You could also use an embellished metal can or a clay vessel. For a creative thinker, thinking outside the book can lead to wonderful, non-traditional interpretations of what a journal can be.

FACING PAGE: Roz Stendahl creates collages out of artifacts from her daily life and keep them in a box. ABOVE LEFT AND RIGHT: Artist Ilira Steinman created this boxed collection of cards for her boyfriend, now husband, to read one card a day while she was away in Italy. BELOW LEFT AND RIGHT: Jeane Minnix's "Wishing Well: Hopes and Dreams."

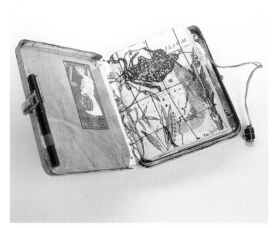

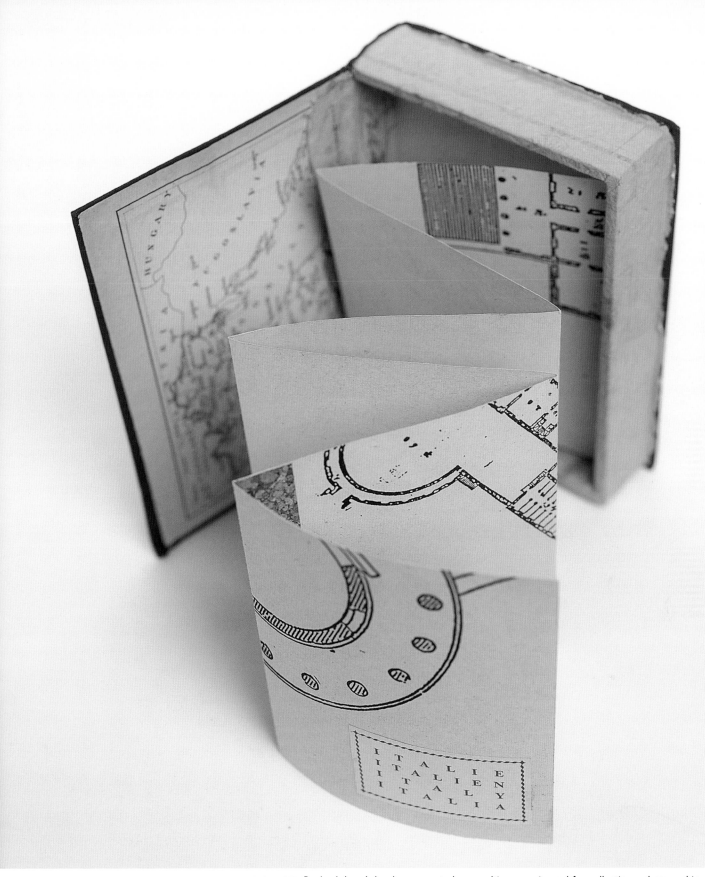

FACING PAGE, TOP AND BOTTOM LEFT: Raphael Lyon's book was created as a multipurpose journal for collecting and researching eth-nobotony in the Brazillilan Rainforest. THIS PAGE AND FACING PAGE, BOTTOM RIGHT: Deborah Naimon says she is drawn to the work of, "Beauty…" and the frayed covers of this vintage book communicates a sense of purpose. Reconstructing the book into a box has given it new life.

Gallery

The following gallery features journals ranging from artists'
sketchbooks and daily journal to books commemorating particular events and places. It isn't often that one is given the opportunity to peek inside personal journals. We hope that the many
examples shown here will serve as visual inspiration for you to
create or continue your own journal.

FACING PAGE: Katy Gilmore's book was created to treasure the richness that comes from the concentrated observances while keeping field notes. LEFT AND BELOW: Dorothy Krause created this journal with collaged materials collected during a trip to Mobile, Alabama and New Orleans, Louisiana over Thanksgiving 1999.

ABOVE LEFT AND MIDDLE LEFT: Jo Bryant describes her books as a safe place to record emotions, ideas, poetry and seeds of ideas for future development.
BELOW AND BOTTOM RIGHT: In 1997 Cheryl Slyter was given a grant to attend the 18th International Conference on Calligraphy and the Lettering Arts. This journal was constructed as a "Thank You" to the Art Center that funded the grant.

BELOW AND BOTTOM: Kimberly Schwenk considered this book a "Big, big risk..." due to the perceived overwhelming size. The challenge to fill the pages kept her going. She describes her book as a narrative journey. RIGHT: Raphael Lyon carried this book around Atlantic City and Providence. It contains, "Love, romance and mysterious travels."

LEFT: The text and images are the primary focus in Kimberly Schwenk's journal. The book deals with issues of loss and broken hearts. The artist used this book to work through her healing process. BOTTOM LEFT AND RIGHT: Dawne Polis created this journal to provide a tangible, visual memory of a wonderful tour with a colleague and fifteen art students. FACING PAGE, TOP: This is a miniature, condensed version of a larger Travel Journal Jane Conneen kept during a trip to Assisi. FACING PAGE, BOTTOM: This book documents Carol Hamoy's thirty happy summers spent on the island of Nantucket, Massachusetts. The island is nicknamed "The Little Grey Lady," thus the title of the book.

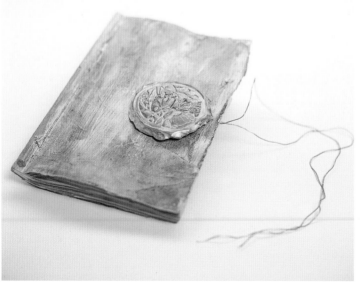

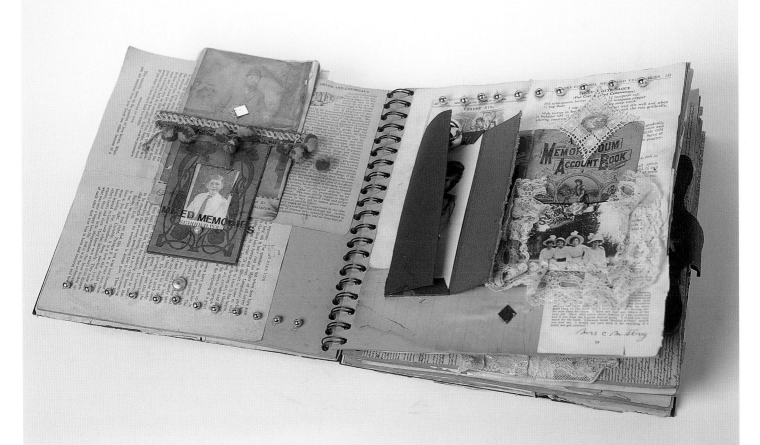

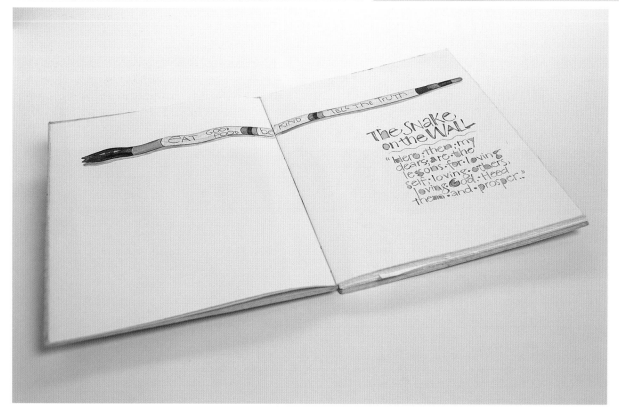

FACING PAGE, TOP LEFT: "Pressure Points" by Wendy Hale Davis who started keeping journals in 1970 because her boyfriend at the time did. Her books have become more intentional and artistic. FACING PAGE, RIGHT AND BOTTOM: This book contains reflections, drawn and written, on small objects—natural and handmade, which Marilyn Reaves loves and responds to—in her immediate environment. ABOVE LEFT: Linnea Montoya started this book in a creative journal making class when she was 17 and used it as a personal creative and mental outlet. ABOVE RIGHT AND LEFT: This book started as a ten year record but was filled in about four years. It contains visual and verbal records of Marilyn R. Rosenberg's 60th - 64th years of life with 'sections' spanning birthday to birthday.

Resources

WHERE TO BUY BLANK BOOKS

Barnes & Noble
1-800-THE-BOOK
www.barnesandnoble.com

Borders Books
1-800-770-7811
www.borders.com

Flax Art & Design
Mail order catalog
240 Valley Drive
Brisbane, CA 94005
415-468-7530
1-800-343-FLAX
www.flaxart.com

Kate's Paperie
561 Broadway
New York, NY 10012
212-941-9816
www.katespaperie.com

Paper Source, Inc.
328 South Jefferson Street, #650
Chicago, IL 60661
312-906-9662

Papyrus
2500 N. Watney Way
Fairfield, CA 94533
1-800-333-6724
www.papyrus-stores.com

Rag & Bone Bindery
Retailers Nationwide
www.ragandbone.com

Rugg Road Paper Company
105 Charles Street
Boston, MA 02114
617-742-0002

Soolip Paperie & Press
11222 Weddington Street
North Hollywood, CA 91601
818-752-0812

Two Hands Paperie
803 Pearl Street
Boulder, CO 80302
303-444-0124
www.twohandspaperie.com

The Written Word
1365 Connecticut Avenue
Washington, DC 20003
202-223-1400

WHERE TO BUY JOURNALING MATERIALS

Art Supply Warehouse
14 Imperial Place
Providence, RI 02906
401-331-4530
Art materials

Pearl Art & Craft
Locations nationwide
www.pearlpaint.com
800-221-6845
art & craft materials

Sam Flax
12 West 20th Street
New York, NY 10011
212-620-3038
Art & design supplies

Beadworks
Locations nationwide
290 Thayer Street
Providence, RI 02906
401-861-4540
Beads and findings

Michael's Crafts
Locations nationwide
972-409-1300
www.michaels.com
Craft materials

The Paper Web
www.artpaper.com
Paper arts
Internet

Nasco
800-558-9595
Art materials
Mail order, catalog available

Dick Blick
800-828-4548
Art materials
Mail order, catalog available

Daniel Smith
800-426-6740
Art materials
Mail order, catalog available

BOOKS ABOUT CREATIVE WRITING

Baldwin, Christina. *Life's Companion: Journal Writing as a Spiritual Quest.* New York: Bantam. 1991.

Baldwin, Christina. *One to One: Self-Understanding through Journal Writing.* New York: M. Evans & Co. 1991.

Bouton, Eldonna. *Loose Ends: A Journaling Tool for Tying up the Incomplete Details of Your Life and Heart.* San Luis Obispo, California: Whole Heart Publications. 1999.

Broyles, Anne. *Journaling: A Spirit Journey.* Nashville, Tennessee: Upper Room Books. 1988.

Cameron, Julia. *The Artist's Way: A Spiritual Path to Higher Creativity.* New York: J.P. Tarcher/Putnam. 1992.

Capacchione, Lucia. *The Creative Journal: The Art of Finding Yourself.* Chicago: Swallow Press. 1979.

Chapman, Joyce. *Journaling for Joy: Writing Your Way to Personal Growth And Freedom.* North Hollywood, California: Newcastle Publications. 1991.

Goldberg, Natalie. *Writing Down the Bones: Freeing the Writer Within.* Boston: Shambhala Publications. 1998.

Holzer, Burghild Nina. *A Walk Between Heaven and Earth: A Personal Journal on Writing and the Creative Process.* New York: Bell Tower. 1994.

Johnson, Dan. *Creative Guide to Journal Writing: How to Enrich Your Life Through Journal Writing.* Louisville, Colorado: Gateway Publications. 1989.

Klauser, Henriette Anne. *Writing on Both Sides of the Brain: Breakthrough Techniques for People Who Write.* San Francisco: Harper. 1987.

Mallon, Thomas. *A Book of One's Own: People and Their Diaries.* St. Paul, Minnesota: Hungry Mind Press. 1995.

Rainer, Tristine. *The New Diary: How to Use a Journal for Self-Guidance and Expanded Creativity.* Preface by Anaïs Nin. New York: G.P. Putnam's Sons. 1978.

Sark. *Living Juicy: Daily Morsels For Your Creative Soul.* Berkeley, California: Celestial Arts. 1994.

Schiwy, Marlene A. *A Voice of Her Own: Women and the Journal-Writing Journey.* New York: Simon and Schuster. 1996.

Simons, George F. *Journal for Life: Discovering Faith and Values Through Journal Keeping.* Chicago: Acta Publications. 1977.

BOOKS ABOUT BOOKBINDING AND JOURNAL-KEEPING

Bannister, Manly. *Craft of Bookbinding.* Dover Publications, 1994

Blake, Kathy. *Handmade Books: A Step-by-Step Guide to Crafting your Own Books.* Bulfinch Press, 1997

Browning, Marie. *Handcrafted Journals, Albums, Scrapbooks, and More.* New York: Sterling Publications. 1999.

Doggett, Sue. *Bookworks: Books, Memory and Photo Albums, Journals, and Diaries Made by Hand.* New York: Watson-Guptill Publications. 1998.

Feliciano, Kristina. *Making Memory Books by Hand: 22 Projects to Make, Keep, and Share.* Gloucester, Massachusetts: Rockport Publishers. 1999.

Ganim, Barbara; Fox, Susan. *Visual Journaling: Going Deeper Than Words.* Wheaton, Illinois: Quest Books. 1999.

Golden, Alisa J. *Creating Handmade Books.* Sterling, 1998

Greenfield, Jane. *ABC of Bookbinding: A Unique Glossary with over 700 Illustrations for Collectors and Librarians.* Oak Knoll Books, 1998

Ikegami, Kojiro. *Japanese Bookbinding.* Weatherhill, New York: Weatherhill Publishers. 1986.

Johnson, Pauline. *Creative Bookbinding.* Dover Publications, 1990

Kenzle, Linda Fry. *Pages: Innovative Book Making Techniques.* Krause, 1998

Lewis, Arthur Williams. *Basic Bookbinding.* Dover Publications, 1985

McCarthy, Mary; Manna, Philip. *Making Books by Hand: A Step-By-Step Guide.* Gloucester, Massachusetts: Rockport Publishers. 1997.

Price, Daniel. *How to Make a Journal of Your Life.* Berkeley, California: Ten Speed Press. 1999.

Richards, Constance. *Making Books and Journals.* Asheville, North Carolina: Lark Books. 1999.

Ryst, Marie. *Handmade Books & Albums: An Introduction to Creative Bookbinding.* Linden Publishing, 1999

Shepard, Rob. *Handmade Books: An Introduction to Bookbinding.* Search Press, 1995

Smith, Keith A. *Bookbinding for Book Artists.* Rochester, New York: Keith Smith Books. 1998.

Smith, Keith A. *Non-Adhesive Binding Books without Paste or Glue.* Rochester, New York: Keith Smith Books. 1999.

Smith, Keith A. *Structure of the Visual Book.* Rochester, New York: Keith Smith Books. 1995.

Smith, Keith A. *Text in the Book Format.* Rochester, New York: Keith Smith Books. 1989.

Zeier, Franz. *Books, Boxes, and Portfolios.* New York: Design Press. 1990.

FACSIMILE JOURNALS

Eldon, Dan; Eldon, Kathy (editor). *The Journey Is the Destination: The Journals of Dan Eldon.* San Francisco: Chronicle Books. 1997.

Jernigan, Candy; Taylor, John Bigelow; Dolphin, Laurie (editor). *Evidence: The Art of Candy Jernigan.* Chronicle Books. 1999.

Harrison, Sabrina Ward. *Spilling Open: The Art of Becoming Yourself.* Novato, California: New World Library. 1999.

Kahlo, Frida; Lowe, Sarah M. (editor); Fuentes, Carlos (introduction). *The Diary of Frida Kahlo: An Intimate Self-Portrait.* New York: Abradale Press. 1998.

Hansen, Beck; Hansen, Al (editor); Baerwaldt, Wayne. *Playing with Matches.* Santa Monica, California: Plug In Editions/Smart Art Press. 1998.

Ohtake, Shinro. *YMCB.* Fukushima, Japan: Center for Contemporary Graphic Art. 1997.

Beard, Peter H. *Beyond the End of the World.* New York: Universe Publishers. 1999.

PUBLICATIONS AND INTERNET RESOURCES

The Artists' Journals Mailing List
http://www.onelist.com/community/artistsjournals
Mailing list & discussion group
One of the most informative visual journal resources on the web

A Capacious Hold-All
32 Fischer Avenue
Islip Terrace, NY 11752
Newsletter focusing on journals and diaries

Conversations Within
www.journalwork.com

Diarist.Net
http://www.diarist.net/
A starting-point for online journals

Journal and Essay Writing
www.poewar.com/links/essay.htm

Journal Jar Ideas
www.omnicron.com/~fluzby/sister-share/journal.htm

Journal Share
www.onelist.com/community/journalshare

Journals and Diaries
207.158.243.119/html/journals___diaries.html

Journal Store
www.journalstore.com

Just Journaling by Joyce Chapman
www.joycechapman.com/journal.html

Keeping Personal Journals
www.uncg.edu/eng/courses/mjabrams/101/diary.htm

LifeTales
members.tripod.com/karenrager/ring.html

Memoirs, Journals, Diaries, Stories
www.wizard.net/~loiselle/story_2.html

Memory & Dream
P.O. Box 103
Slippery Rock, PA 16057
'Zine with an emphasis on journals and journal-keeping

Metajournals
www.metajournals.com

The National Journal Network
http://www.geocities.com/SoHo/9993/
An active group of committed diarists

Open Pages
www.hedgehog.net/op/

Personal Journaling
www.journalingmagazine.com

The Scribe Tribe
www.myplanet.net/bdalporto

The Secret Diary
http://www.spies.com/~diane/journals.html
Lessons, history, and resources for journalers

The Studio
39570 SE Park Street, #201
Snoqualmie, WA 98065
'Zine with journaling topics and art

Suite 101: Journal Writing
www.suite101.com/welcome.cfm/journal_writing

Thrive's Online Journal Writing Program
thriveonline.aol.com/serenity.journal/index.html

20th Century Women (e-zine)
www.20thcenturywomen.com

Writing the Journey
http://www.writingthejourney.com/
Journal writing exercises and resources

Contributors

THANK YOU TO ALL THE ARTISTS
WHO PARTICIPATED IN THIS PROJECT!

Rag & Bone Bindery
One Allens Avenue
Providence, RI 02903
www.ragandbone.com
Bookbinding studio creating hand-bound
journals and more. Established in 1991.
Wholesale only.

The Paper Source
328 South Jefferson Street, #650
Chicago, IL 60661
312-906-9662
Handmade papers and cards, rubber
stamps, book-binding and journaling supplies and blank books of all kinds

Betty Auchard
115 Belhaven Drive
Los Gatos, CA 95032
408-356-8224
btauchard@aol.com

Jo Bryant
630 Graceland Drive SE
Albuquerque, NM 87108

James Castle
Reproduction of all Castle images courtesy
of the A. C. Wade Estate, Castle Collection,
L. P.

Janis Cheek
8621 Hahn Street
Utica, MI 48317

Elizabeth Clark
1505 West Willetta Street
Phoenix, AZ
mussaku@hotmail.com
Proprietor of Mussaku, a shop specializing
in hand-made books, boxes, and portfolios

Maura Cluthe
4514 Cambridge Street
Kansas City, KS 66103
fragmented@earthlink.net

Juliana Coles
829 San Lorenzo NW
Albuquerque, NM 87107
www.meandpete.com

Jane Conneen
The Little Farm Press
820 Andrews Road
Bath, PA 18014
610-759-5326
lfarmpress@aol.com

Evelyn Eller
71-49 Harrow Street
Forest Hills, NY 11375
eller-rosenbaum@worldnet.att.net

Katy Gilmore
1555 H Street
Anchorage, AK 99501

Wendy Hale Davis
40 Crockett Street
Austin, TX 78704
worldbridger@earthlink.net

Carol Hamoy
340 East 66th Street
New York, NY 10021

Sherri Keisel
114 Paintbrush Street
Lake Jackson, TX 77566
sherites@aol.com

Kimberly Koufax
P.O. Box 8683
Portland, OR 97207
haystackart@aol.com

Dorothy Simpson Krause
32 Nathaniel Way
P.O. Box 421
Marshfield Hills, MA 02051
781-837-1682
www.dotkrause.com

Bruce Kremer
P.O. Box 2458
Ketchum, ID 83340
www.bkremer.com

Roberta Lavadour
48006 Saint Andrew's Road
Pendleton, OR 97801
www.papertrails.com

L.K. Ludwig
P.O. Box 103
Slippery Rock, PA 16057
724-266-5643
lkludwig@home.com

Raphael Lyon
67 Barclay Road
Clintondale, NY 12515
Bookbinder specializing in heirloom gifts

Sally Mac Namara-Ivey
848 East Main Street
Sheridan, OR 97378
503-843-5598
sivey@onlinemac.com

Peter Madden
109 F Street
Boston, MA 02127
617-269-5284
boyauboy@aol.com

Jeanne Minnix
6401 Academy Road NE, #69
Albuquerque, NM 87109
jminnix@griffinassoc.com

Linnea Montoya
2025 Palomas Drive NE
Albuquerque, NM 87110
505-265-6874
linnyag@hotmail.com

Teesha Moore
39570 SE Park Street, #201
Snoqualmie, WA 98065

Tracy Moore
39570 SE Park Street, #201
Snoqualmie, WA 98065

Maria Pisano
6 Titu Lane
Plainsboro, NJ 08536
mgpstudio@aol.com

Dawne Polis
1348 Mad Tom Road
East Dorset, VT 05253
ddcpolis@vermontel.net

Marilyn Reaves
1260 West 15th Avenue, #6
Eugene, OR 97402
541-485-7862
mreaves@darkwing.uoregon.edu

Marilyn Rosenberg
67 Lakeview Avenue West
Cortlandt Manor, NY 10567
914-737-2052

Kimberly Schwenk
203 Girard Boulevard SE
Albuquerque, NM 87106
505-232-6648
kschwenk@unm.edu

Judith Serebrin
420 Arch Street
Redwood City, CA 94062
650-364-1659
serebrin@pacbell.net

Melissa Slattery
255 South Avenue
New Canaan, CT 06840
wrslattery@snet.net

Cheryl Slyter
26100 Hawthorne Drive
Franklin, MI 48025
248-737-1932
slyter@oeonline.com

Polly Smith
1047 North Lombard Avenue
Oak Park, IL 60302
708-524-8194
pilpol@aol.com

Elizabeth Steiner
P.O. Box 60 026
29 Kohu Road
Titirangi, Auckland 1230
New Zealand
steiner@iprolink.co.nz

Ilira Steinman
One Allens Avenue
Providence, RI 02903
401-455-3680
www.ragandbone.com
Artist, milliner and co-owner of Rag &
Bone Bindery, Providence, Rhode Island

Roz Stendahl
630 Huron Boulevard SE
Minneapolis, MN 55414
roslyn.m.stendhal-1@tc.umn.edu

Jeffree Stewart
P.O. Box 7397
Olympia, WA 98507
360-754-1486
jste461@ecy.wa.gov

Jason Thompson
One Allens Avenue
Providence, RI 02903
401-455-3680
www.ragandbone.com
Journaler and owner of Rag & Bone
Bindery, Providence, Rhode Island

Kez Van Oudheusden
30 Brooke Street
Clayfield, Australia Q4011
061-7-3862-4074
kez@eis.net.au

Deborah Waimon
1 Cherry Hill Lane
New Milford, CT 06776

Anne Woods
986 Botsford Road
Ferrisburgh, VT 05456
maasalama@hotmail.com

Index

the Author

Jason Thompson is the founder and president of Rag & Bone Bindery in Providence, Rhode Island, the largest, private hand-bookbinding studio in America solely creating handbound blank books, albums, and journals for the gift and stationery industries. He began journal writing in 1986 while spending a year walking across the country from Los Angeles, California to Washington, D.C. on the Great Peace March, and has been keeping visual journals ever since. He currently resides in Providence, Rhode Island.